What causes a person to commit suicide? David Wilkerson believes it is because his search for the meaning of life has left him confused and bitter. SUICIDE discusses how self-destructive thoughts begin and how we can recognize these symptoms before it is too late. It points out God's ideas concerning suicide by citing relevant biblical passages. Most of all, it shows how to permanently fill the void that causes despair, depression, and loneliness.

BY David Wilkerson

The Cross and the Switchblade
Beyond the Cross and the Switchblade
The Little People
Man, Have I Got Problems
Twelve Angels From Hell
Hey, Preach . . . You're Comin' Through!
Parents on Trial
Rebel's Bible
Purple Violet Squish
David Wilkerson Speaks Out
I'm Not Mad at God
Racing Toward Judgment
The Vision
Life on the Edge of Time
My Bible Speaks to Me
Pocket Promise Book
End Times New Testament
Jesus Person Maturity Manual
Jesus Christ Solid Rock
Sipping Saints
Suicide

SUICIDE

David Wilkerson

SPIRE BOOKS

Fleming H. Revell Company
Old Tappan, New Jersey

Scripture quotations are based on the King James Version of the Bible.

Library of Congress Cataloging in Publication Data

Wilkerson, David R
   Suicide.

   SUMMARY: Shows teenagers how to establish
communication with God to overcome the tormenting
problems driving thousands of them to suicide each
year.
    1.   Youth—Suicidal behavior—Juvenile literature.
2.   Youth—Religious behavior—Juvenile literature.
3.   Suicide—Prevention—Juvenile literature.
[1. Suicide. 2. Christian life] I. Title.
HV6546.W54   362.2   78-19052
ISBN 0-8007-8331-X

A Spire Book
Copyright © 1978 by World Challenge, Inc.,
and Fleming H. Revell Company
Published by Fleming H. Revell Company
with David Wilkerson Publications
All rights reserved
Printed in the United States of America
This is an original Spire Book, published by Spire Books,
a Division of Fleming H. Revell Company
Old Tappan, New Jersey

Contents

Preface

I hope there is something in this book for everyone thinking of suicide and for those who want to help.

The Bible warns we must do everything within our power to stop suicidals from attempting to take their lives. ". . . deliver them that are drawn unto death . . . ready to be slain" (Proverbs 24:11). "Open thy mouth for the dumb in the cause of all such as are appointed to destruction" (Proverbs 31:8).

I had to write this book about suicide. I had no other choice. Too many teenagers are killing themselves. They send me written confessions and suicide threats. They come forward in our crusades, crying for help. Suicide is the second biggest killer of youth in this nation, second only to auto accidents. And many of those accidents should have been listed as suicides. Drunken, pill-crazed students have discovered the car can be a lethal weapon—a way to commit suicide without shaming their parents.

Writing this book has deeply affected me, and I will never be the same. I discovered how little I know about troubled people. But then, God's precious Word began to unfold, and I discovered how much the Bible has to say about suicide.

You will sense the compelling power of God's Word, as you read about men of God who stood at the brink of death and came back. Job's victory over the fatal urge is a thrilling example.

Best of all, God is shining His light into the dark minds of suicidals. Thousands are now being plucked out of Satan's death grip. Bodies, as well as souls, are being saved.

1

Suicide—The Fatal Urge

The Holy Spirit has been prompting me to speak out about suicide. At first I rebelled against preaching about such a morbid subject, but there was no way I could shake the urgency to warn young people about the horror of self-destruction. Consequently, I have been preaching about suicide in our city-wide crusades and have sent out thousands of booklets to awaken young people.

Now I know why God put this message in my heart! Last year this nation experienced a 200 percent increase in youth suicides. Thousands of teenagers have killed themselves, and hundreds of thousands of young adults attempt suicide each year. It is fast becoming the number-one killer of youth in our country, second only to auto accidents.

I have been shocked to tears each night that I preach on suicide. Numbers of young people come forward at our invitation to receive Christ as Lord of their lives. They are always honest in confessing their problems.

I wanted to know why God prompted me to speak out on this subject, so I have been asking the question, "How many of you standing before me have been thinking of taking your life?" Each time I asked this pointed question, at least 10 percent of them raised their hands in confession. This means anywhere from twenty to forty young people in each group were flirting with suicide. Of that number, five to ten confessed they were planning suicide within the day or week.

There Is an Epidemic of Suicides

In all my years of preaching to troubled youth, I have never been as shaken and sorrowed as I have been in learning of all these mixed-up kids wanting to destroy themselves.

In Dallas, Texas, a bank president stepped out in his front yard to get the morning paper. He turned toward the house, horrified—there on the upper porch was his son, hanging by the neck. The boy was a drug addict, who came to the conclusion suicide was the only way out.

Repentant teenagers confess their suicidal urges to me. One fifteen-year-old girl cried out, "My mother killed herself, and I couldn't forgive her. So I decided tonight was the night to get even with her by killing myself. I've lived with anger and hate every day since she died. But tonight Jesus took away my hate. I will never kill myself now. Jesus has given me a new hope!"

Another teenager confessed, through her tears, "My drug-addicted brother was murdered. I loved him so much. I got mad at God for allowing it to happen. Suicide was going to be my way of getting back at God for being a killer. But not anymore. Your message was meant just for me—to save my life. I forgive! Never again will I allow Satan to make suicide look attractive. It's all over. I am going with Jesus now!"

One teenage boy jumped up during a counseling session, pulled out a knife, and cried, "This is the knife! It was going to be tonight! My life is filled with fear and loneliness! I want to be saved and set free from these thoughts of suicide."

I rushed a counselor to him, to grab the knife. He surrendered it willingly and fell to his knees, limp and sobbing. Three young people from his high school ran to his side and began to pray with him. Not only did that boy get a new lease on life, he left the meeting with three newly made friends to help him overcome his loneliness.

What Is Causing This Wave of Suicides?

There are many causes of suicide among the young who come to us for help. One of the prime causes is the despair of enslavement to an addiction.

Drug addicts, alcoholics, and homosexuals are all candidates for suicide. Thousands of young people are hooked by demonic habits that have ruined their lives. They look in the mirror one morning, horrified! They see the sunken cheeks, the deep, dark rings under their eyes, and the emaciated arms and legs. They feel the hurt and sickness inside. Then they think of how they are destroying themselves and their parents. Most of them still love their parents, and they become overwhelmed with guilt and sorrow for all the torment and misery they have caused them. Suicide seems to be the only escape left.

One young addict confessed, "I've ruined my life. I was innocent and tender just a few years ago. I was that average, respectable teenager who did all the right things. But I got in with the wrong crowd, got hooked on drugs, and now look at me. My parents have lost respect for me. Mom looks at me and just breaks out crying. I know I'm just like an animal now. I have no reason to live. I'm tired of hurting myself, and I'm sick of making my parents suffer so much. I know they die a little each day when they see how much I've changed. Maybe when they stand in front of my casket, they can forgive me and remember me the way I used to be."

So many times I have parents in my office, crying out deep hurts caused when they discovered their children were hooked or perverted.

Recently a respectable, middle-aged Christian couple confessed, "Just this week our son confessed to us he is a practicing homosexual. We tried to share our hurt with our daughter, and she dropped a second bombshell on us. She admitted she is a lesbian. We are so deeply hurt, we don't know how to react. We are almost numb with anxiety. We don't even know how to talk to them now. They are our only children, and both are mixed-up. But we still love them. What do we do now?"

When I questioned those heartbroken parents further, I

11

discovered both the son and daughter also carried deep hurts. They hated what had happened to them. They especially hated causing hurt and confusion to their parents. I began to feel compassion not only for the father and mother, but also for the poor son and daughter trapped in such terrifying habits. These students were on the brink of suicide. And, because those parents still loved them, that just added to the despair of their son and daughter.

The hooked teenager wants to kill himself (herself) to atone for his sin. He thinks, "I am a failure. I deserve to die." It's a form of self-crucifixion. They want to go to their cross, like Jesus did, and pay for sin. They don't seem to know Jesus already paid for it all.

Divorce and Broken Homes

Another major cause of teenage suicide is a broken home. Last year there were more than one million new divorces, with ten million kids victimized by these and previous divorces. On the Judgment Day, I see a generation of lonely, mixed-up kids rising to witness against parents whom they believe let them down.

The prophet Isaiah must have been thinking of our broken homes when he said, "Prepare slaughter for his children for the iniquity of their fathers . . ." (Isaiah 14:21).

Splitting, breaking-up parents are provoking children to unbelievable anger. In Denton, Texas, sits a fourteen-year-old mute girl, who refuses to talk or to move. She was once an outgoing, happy girl, who idolized her parents. But one day her dad just walked out and moved in with another woman. That very day, Margie crawled into a shell and has not spoken a word since. I can't reach her. Nobody can. She is in her room as if deaf and mute. One day she may choose to end it all. And that father will stand before God on Judgment Day and answer for that ruined teenager's life—as will thousands of parents who divorced without concern for their children.

Not all children of broken homes and divorce are mixed-up and on the verge of suicide. But sometimes it doesn't show up until years later. We now counsel with young marrieds who trace their depression back to their childhood years. They felt rejected and cheated when their parents divorced. Even when teenagers, they put up a good front to cover their hurt. But then one day, years later, the hurt and hate explode in many directions. Their marriages suffer. And, all too often, they begin to flirt with suicide. Their seething anger finally poisons their marriages, years later.

I was shocked by the flood of mail I received after sending out a letter about teenage suicide. My letter was sent to nearly one-half million people. Here are just a few samples of the many letters I received as a result. Reading them, you will get a clearer picture as to why so many are flirting with suicide. I share them just as I received them, unedited. They tell of broken homes; broken hearts; addictions; troubled marriages; isolation from friends, family, and God; and of overwhelming problems of all kinds.

- I thought your message on suicide was very good and interesting. You see, I slit my wrist twice last year. I wanted to die, but I was too scared to do it. I just wanted out, because everyone in my school was going out on dates when they were 14, and I have to wait until I'm 16 (this March). They figured every time I went out, I'd get drunk and "do something I'd regret later" because that was how my sisters were. They didn't trust me at all and soon my boyfriend dropped me 'cuz he could never see me. I felt terrible, it was all their fault (parents), so I slit my wrist. It wasn't serious at all, so they never found out. They usually won't have too much to do with me. Then I found someone else who then got bored and left. So I did it again, but he came back and said he was sorry. And we've been

13

together for eight months now. I love him so much, and he loves me, too, and I'm so glad I didn't die. In your message you talked about Janet who felt terrible when she lost her boyfriend, so she killed herself. I, too, was in that position and tried to kill myself but I didn't succeed, and I'm really glad to be here. I wish to God that I could have been there to help Janet. I think about her often. Keep up the good work; you're sending many young people the right way. It must be a great feeling!

Love,
J.S.R.

• As I read your letter and your paper on suicide, it made me weep inside. That word struck a dagger in my heart because only recently I wrote to you for prayer for a young man, my first cousin, who had overdosed on pills and almost lost his life. God let a miracle happen. You wrote me and sent literature for him; he read it, and began to read the Bible. He told his family God let him see where he had gone wrong, how he had hurt so many, and that he was convicted of his sins. He was on the verge of complete surrender to God, but now he's forever gone. He took a sawed off shotgun and blew his brains out. He had an argument with his girl friend. He slapped her—she took out a warrant—the police pursued him. From there he was as a wild man. He held two police at gunpoint then ran and barricaded himself in his father's home, held him at gunpoint, then finally ran and locked himself in his room. The dad pleaded with him, but it was too late. The shot sounded. The dad crashed through the door, only to see a horrible mess, what only minutes before was a nice looking son. Even in that condition, he lived about eight hours, never to gain consciousness. It consoles me to know your prayers did help him, yet I've asked, "Oh God, why did I not try harder to talk to him, even pray with him, when the

14

opportunity was there?" He might have broken down. Now he's gone! Please pray for his mother and dad. They're getting old. Also the brothers and sisters— they're all backsliders.

Sincerely,
J.N.

- I am 15 and in a sense your ministry saved me. Lately I've been going through a lot. My parents are not Christians and neither are my brothers and sisters. My parents travel a lot because of my father's job. I'm the oldest girl, so I have to take care of the family. Also, I've been having boyfriend trouble. I love him so much that when we broke up I went into a state of depression. Last night I was ready to commit suicide, but then I decided to put it off and let God handle it. God came through. I've come out of my depression, and things are great.

B.N.

- Your article on teenage suicide touched me deeply. Remembering about a friend of mine two years ago that committed suicide. His grades in school dropped, troubles with students and his parents. It's a shame. Not many people showed up at his funeral, but at least he could of had Jesus as a friend. Or he would be alive today. Sometimes things just happen too late! I'm alive and well and don't ever plan to commit suicide for the sake of my soul.

S.M.J.

- After ten and one-half years of troubled marriage, separating, getting back together, my husband finally shot himself through the head. Your letter is the best thing I've read on suicide. I only wish someone had said it sooner. I know it will help others.

A.L.

- The message on suicide couldn't have come at a better time, for ten minutes before my brother brought me the mail, I was contemplating which way I should do it. I tried to kill myself this summer but my friend caught me. You said how it wouldn't be the end—judgment and darkness, but what about a backslidden Christian? I am curious, would God send me to hell for it? Take care and please write me and answer my questions if you have a minute or two sometime.

  B.F.

- Your letter about suicide really blessed my heart. You see, one woman from our Bible study group attempted suicide with 150 pills and a bottle of vodka. They revived her. Three weeks later she was back in psychopath ready and eager to take her life again. Led by the Lord, I went and witnessed to her. That very night she gave her life to Christ and is now working for the Lord, a completely healed woman.

  P.T.

- Three years ago I was on the brink of suicide. I was a speed freak on the verge of alcoholism. Then Jesus Christ came into my life and set me free. I certainly am not the same girl today!

  R.L.

- Your last message on suicide really hit home with me. I'm from a broken home and I was running away and taking drugs most of my teen years. Then I quit drugs, got married, had a beautiful baby girl, then ended up divorced. I'm new in Christ and I'm trying but I guess somehow I've been letting myself think about suicide. I thought I'd be forgiven. Praise the Lord for your message. I'm putting suicide out of my mind, and I'm going to concentrate on the Lord and raising my daughter in Jesus.

  J.K.

- Your letter on suicide arrived Wednesday, just an hour or so after I was informed that a high school junior I know is suicidal. I was grateful for the letter, not only because it made me aware of the situation, but I believe it can be used by God. As a substitute teacher, I've noticed that many, many kids writing term papers have chosen suicide as a topic. Tomorrow I will put your letter in the library with the reference books used to write these papers. I know the Lord will use your paper to speak to the right kids.

  S.C.L.

- Yes, I know all too well the heartbreak of suicide. I stood over the dying body of a beloved granddaughter who had poured a gallon of gasoline over her body and set herself on fire. She lived long enough to give me the assurance that she was saved. It was an experience I shall never forget. Her words still ring in my ears, "Grandma, how long will it take me to die?" I did not pray for her to live; she wanted so much to die. And though she could not speak to me I know she had found the Savior in those days of dying. Now I have another granddaughter on the same road. Please pray for her! I pray constantly and so do her parents.

  C.O.

- Mr. Wilkerson, my wife and I received your message on suicide in the mail. We attended your services when you were at Kennewick High School, Kennewick, Washington. I know there was a message in it for me because I was thinking about suicide that very night we attended that service. The devil was playing with my life through alcohol and the fear of death made me want to get it over with sooner. But that same night I gave my life to Christ; I don't boast of myself but for the glory of God.

  J.J.L.

17

- Your message on suicide really touched me. I was very depressed last year and thought of suicide even though I was a Christian. I even prayed for God to let me die, just like Moses and Elijah and Jonah did. Well, He didn't answer their prayers and praise God, He didn't answer mine. There really is a way out. Now I have a lot to live for. My fiance also has had the same problem. He is prone to severe depression. He is a new believer and seems to be learning to trust God.

    T.V.E.

- Your message didn't even penetrate me about suicide. Suicide just stays on my mind. Jesus doesn't even seem to be a reality. Maybe I'm ashamed of Him. But it won't make any difference if I did die or not because I need a relationship with Jesus and all the relationships with any person are unreal myth. It's already like I don't really exist. One time I was wishing I was dead and all by myself and almost fell off a cliff (got too close) and decided I didn't want to die that badly. But I'm not chicken to give up something I don't have anyway!

    D.Y.

- I received your message on suicide today. It is something—of all times. My son just yesterday told me he was going to kill himself. I talked to him and told him that wouldn't end it. That he would not go to heaven and be with God. That it is the devil's work. That's what he wants people to do—destroy themselves. I am leaving this message lay on my table so he can read it also. Please pray for my family.

    S.E.U.

- I just wanted to write because I read your letter on suicide and it really got to me. Because when I was a teenager, just a few years back, I tried to commit suicide a lot of times. I was on drugs and drank for most of my precious teenage years. I was even put in a state mental hospital for wanting to kill myself. I got pregnant when I was 18 and I was all alone. My sister is a Christian and had told me a year earlier how I could know Jesus but I just wouldn't. After my baby was born, I cried out to God to help me. My baby is two and a half, and I have grown to love Jesus more every day. So I know that Jesus can save. I pray that you can reach some of these kids before they do take their lives.

B.L.

My daughter contemplated suicide. She even wrote a letter of a last will and even checked on the price of funerals, so I learned from one of her girl friends. One evening I came to the house and she had it locked and all the gas jets and oven running without flames. It shook me. I called in a minister to help and she came out of her bedroom like it was just a lark—but it was no lark to me! Since a prayer of healing between us, at least we can communicate on the natural level now. For one of her term papers, my daughter researched suicide and reported on it—but it was only on the worldly level, not what the Bible says about suicide to murdering. Now she is married and has a little girl herself. Shortly after the little girl was born, I told her that as she loves her little daughter, so I loved her so she told me she knew that. I'm praying for the day of her salvation.

A.A.G.

I know what you are saying about suicide is true. I had often contemplated taking my life as an easy way out. But I got the same message you are now preaching directly from God. I tremble a little to think how many kids my age have killed themselves. Some of my

19

friends even have attempted suicide. They miraculously lived and some are now Christians.

T.E.

- Your message to me concerning suicide touched my heart. I feel both for those that take their lives and for those close to them who will always ask why. Being from a broken home, I, too, have experienced the feelings of bitterness and despair that make suicide attractive. But, praise God, I was aware of what God says about life, death, and judgment. And with Jesus, I can forgive and experience real love.

J.L.

- I'm not into drugs or alcohol but I've thought about taking my life. It's just that depression sets in and it's hard to find a reason to live (although I have plenty). But the thing that always stopped me is that I'm not sure where I'm going and I know death is not the end. I feel I've committed the ultimate sin by turning my back on Christ and I don't want to die because I'm almost sure I'm going to hell. At this point, I don't feel like I'll ever lead a Christian life because of peer pressure and lack of Christians around.

B.B.C.

- I am so thankful for your letter that I just received. I read it and was deeply hurt that so many kids my age are committing suicide. Not long after I had read your letter—the next day, in fact—I received a phone call from my friend. I knew she had been having problems and I had been praying for her. She is pregnant and unmarried. Her father had given her three choices: marry the baby's father, get an abortion, or move out. I was shocked and heartbroken. I didn't know what to say to her. Then she said, "Maybe it would just be better if I killed myself and finished all my problems." I told her no, that's not going to help. She explained that no one really cared for her. I told her I cared and

20

God cared. I think I got her to change her mind about committing suicide.

L.H.

● Your message on suicide touched me deeply, and I know the burden you feel. Five years ago my husband committed suicide at the age of twenty-two. He and I were both alcoholics and with that problem and others, he felt as though that was the only way of escape. But, praise God! He used that tragic circumstance as a means to bring me and others to His blessed Son. I know God is going to use you to get this message out, and I, along with others, will be praying.

B.D.

● I have a daughter that is on drugs and she has said that no one loves her. She says she wants to die. I have talked and done everything that I know.

J.R.C.

● You've finally touched on something I can identify with. You see, I am a would-be suicide. Praise God I don't have to fight off that urge anymore. What leads to suicide? *Depression.* Depression so bad you go to bed hoping you'll never wake up, only to face nightmares all night long. So you wake up reluctantly, regretting another day, consoling yourself with the thought you'd be dead by evening and you went home to face "that" again. Only you aren't unless you "do something."

Yes, I heard rumors that God didn't like us to take our own lives. But no one could find a single Bible verse that said precisely that. Yes, I see the 1 Corinthians 3:16, 17 you quoted. It would not have convinced me then. I was too depressed. What held me back? Only God's grace. I ended up under doctor's care. Sometimes the "medical help" makes life even less bearable. I was schizophrenic and some of those medicines only weakened my defenses against those conflicting, distorting thoughts and sensations that bombarded my mind constantly. I read "The People," on science fiction and "Suicide." There the norm looked on death as returning to the Creator and suicide as returning with your work unfinished.

I agree now there seems to be a special darkness for successful suicide. I read somewhere of some would-be suicides exposed to this. He changed his mind. I've also read this concept. God has a plan for everyone of us. A goal, as it were. How fast we reach that goal depends on how willing we are to try for it. God is patient. If we drag our heels, so to speak, He has lots of time. But if we kill ourselves, our time is gone. We can never become what we were created to be and part of God's plan is destroyed. You see what an advantage a suicide would be to Satan?

What will break the urge? Well, guessing from your examples, forgiveness. But somehow that wouldn't have stopped those prevailing distortions. I needed healing. The Baptism? God did wonders but still I "healed slowly." What broke the "suicide urge"? Pure, reasonless, objectless praise. One day after I had received the Baptism of the Holy Spirit, the urge came more strongly than it had ever been. I was vividly aware that the river was within walking distance of my home. I was home alone. No one would stop me until too late. But I finally had reason to live. Well, I went out that Spring day to spade in the garden. My "temple" was in high gear. Nothing was right. I knew I should try praise. But with my "complainer" in full gear, I couldn't think of anything worth praising anyone for. I was alone, so I dared to sing. I chose the 8-fold "Allelujah" because it was praise but didn't need a reason to praise. In the meantime, I spaded. It took all morning, but when the urge left, it also "lifted" me. I've never had to fight it off since. Hallelujah!

D.R.C.

• I want to die! Three times in the last month I tried to commit suicide; I failed! I've gone from trying to overdose to slitting my wrist. Last night I called the cops for help. They had to take the knife from me. I tried to cut myself, but couldn't break the skin. I lie here now wanting to die. It's hard for me to talk to anyone. I tried talking to a preacher; I guess it didn't work. I'm afraid of the next time I try this. Please help me. I'm only 21—too young to die. I don't want to spend my life trying to kill myself. I don't know what to do. I can't stand to stay this way. I hate life and I want out, but God won't let me go. Please help me somehow. I used to be a happy-go-lucky Christian, now I dread waking up each day. I know it will happen again if you can't help me. Please, anyone, help me!

B.I.A.

2

"I Really Don't Want to Die!"

Suicide is a very dangerous game, and it is often played by people who really don't want to die. The potential of unintentional death is in every suicide attempt. Lonely, sad, and depressed, many do not know how to reach out for help. They don't want to keep on living the way they are, yet they don't want to end up as a corpse.

The majority of teenage boys and men who commit suicide do it with explosives and guns. The second most common method is hanging, followed closely by overdosing with narcotics. Girls and women most frequently kill themselves with pills, guns, and by hanging, in that order.

People who don't really want to die usually don't try violent methods. Guns, explosives, hanging, jumping from high places are all too dangerous for them. They know it will probably end in certain death. Instead, they take just enough pills to knock themselves out, without killing. Or, they will slash a wrist or arm, making sure it is only a surface wound. They want to bleed without dying. This also allows plenty of "rescue time." If they do use a gun, they just graze themselves enough to leave severe and noticeable powder burns. They leave suicide notes where they can be found, hoping someone will take them seriously and talk them out of it.

Nobody plays these kinds of games unless they are really crying for help. And suicide talk is not something that a person just outgrows. Too often, family and friends think it is a way of getting attention and they dismiss it by saying, "Oh, he would never do such a thing." Or, "She's too chicken. It's just a lot of talk. She's just trying to make us pity her." Sadly, thousands who talk about suicide wind up in a morgue.

Most people who talk about attempting suicide want to be talked out of it. It is not so much that they want to go on living, but rather that they are afraid to die. Deep within them lingers a fear of eternity. They have just enough religious training to make them worry about ending in hell, should they kill themselves. The thought that suicide may be an unpardonable sin keeps nagging at their consciences.

There are many today who toy with thoughts of suicide without ever telling anyone else. They abhor the very word. But the thought of an easy escape keeps popping up in their minds. One woman confessed, "I knew I was not so stupid to ever kill myself, but when things in my marriage got really bad, I would have these fleeting thoughts about ending it all just to get even with him."

As many as one million now attempt suicide each year. Teachers tell me a growing number of students are studying the subject and are writing about suicide for term papers.

The Bible says, "For as he thinketh in his heart, so is he . . ." (Proverbs 23:7). Job said, "For the thing I greatly feared is come upon me . . ." (Job 3:25). These and many other Scriptures point out the dangers of allowing such thoughts to roam about freely in the mind. These are the kinds of thoughts Paul was warning us to be ". . . bringing into captivity every thought to the obedience of Christ" (2 Corinthians 10:5).

Thoughts are like seeds; they grow. In a climate of loneliness and depression, these little seeds can grow into life-consuming roots that twist all through the mind. Our thoughts can rule the body. Thoughts have a way of becoming words, and words become deeds. The Bible suggests death and life are in the power of the tongue. "Death and life are in the power of the tongue: and they that love it shall eat the fruit thereof" (Proverbs 18:21).

Suicide is in the power of the tongue. So is life. This means, simply, power to live or die is in the mind. Because, ". . . of the abundance of the heart his

26

mouth speaketh'' (Luke 6:45).

Do not allow these thoughts to remain. Ask the Holy Spirit to sweep them out. Fill your mind with the Word of God. Paul summed it up like this:

> Finally, brethren, whatsoever things are true, whatsoever things are honest, whatsoever things are just, whatsoever things are pure, whatsoever things are lovely, whatsoever things are of good report; if there be any virtue, and if there be any praise, think on these things.
>
> Philippians 4:8

3

Suicide—An Unpardonable Sin

Few people today understand God's attitude toward suicide. Many of those rescued from an attempted suicide say they thought death was the end of everything. To them, suicide was considered an easy and attractive way to escape from overwhelming problems. As one teenager put it, "What could be wrong about taking your own life, if it is worthless to you? When you die, you just float away on a peaceful cloud into nothingness."

Another said, "When you die, you just die. It's a world of peace and tranquility. It's the end of all your hassles and troubles. No one can hurt you after you die."

This generation is in the throes of a terrible satanic deception. It is deceived into thinking self-imposed death is a moral right of every human being. "It's my body, and I can do with it as I please. I'm not hurting anybody but myself. My fate is in my own hands."

Death has been romanticized as some kind of a "beautiful journey into a world of dazzling color and supreme peace." Teenagers who come down from an overdose tell stories about seeing angels; about hovering over their bodies, observing life, while their spirits soared freely about as eagles; about brilliant colors and fleecy, white clouds. Death becomes a kind of spiritual Disney World.

To this generation, death is not an enemy. It has lost its sting. Instead, death is the ultimate trip—an adventure to be desired. Young people today have seen people die a thousand ways on television and in movies.

Death has come to so many of their schoolmates, it is almost commonplace. Across the nation, students have learned to nonchalantly accept deaths of thousands of classmates, who died from overdoses, from auto accidents due to drunk driving, and from suicides. There even seems to be a sigh of relief when a troubled student dies, as if to say, "Well, at least nobody can hurt him now. He is beyond the reach of danger."

Death Is Not the End

The Bible says, ". . . after death, the judgment" (*see* Hebrews 9:27). People who commit suicide do not just die and then decay into nothingness. Death is not the end at all; it is just the beginning. Every suicide victim goes straight to the judgment hall of Christ, to answer to Him for rejecting His priceless gift of life. No one can play God by taking his life. No one will ever be permitted to throw that life back into God's face. No one will be permitted to abort God's divine plan for his life. No one will be allowed to go into eternity with his life's work undone, without being judged as a thief.

Your Body Does Not Belong to You!

Jesus Christ paid a high price for the legal and moral ownership of every human body. The mortgage on your body belongs only to Him. He died a criminal's death to purchase both body and soul.

> What? know ye not that your body is the temple of the Holy Ghost which is in you . . . and ye are not your own? For ye are bought with a price: therefore glorify God in your body, and in your spirit, which are God's.
>
> 1 Corinthians 6:19, 20

When a person commits suicide, he is robbing God. "Will a man rob God?" (*See* Malachi 3:8.) God alone holds the keys to life and death, and only He has the right to usher a soul into eternity.

"But I can't worry about that," a coed told me. "This is my problem; it's my body, my future; it's my life—and

30

no one else has anything to say about it. I'll just have to take my chances."

The Bible says, "If any man defile the temple of God, him shall God destroy . . ." (1 Corinthians 3:17). Furthermore, we are commanded in God's Word to preserve our bodies for Him. ". . . I pray God your whole spirit and soul and body be preserved blameless unto the coming of our Lord Jesus Christ" (1 Thessalonians 5:23).

Only People Who Have Lost Their Fear of God Commit Suicide

Every time I hear of another person committing suicide, I think to myself, "They could have never pulled that trigger—they would not have swallowed those pills—in no way could they have killed themselves—if they knew it was an unpardonable sin—and that people who destroy their lives must answer to God on the Judgment Day."

An elderly missionary heard me preach about suicide, and she asked to talk after the meeting. She said, "David, I thank God you are dealing with this serious problem. But when you listed all the reasons why people kill themselves, you forgot to mention the greatest deterrent there is against suicide. It is the fear of God. When I was a teenager, my Methodist minister father got it through my head that suicide was a terrible sin and people who destroy themselves go to hell. You may not agree with that, but my generation didn't even think of suicide, because we had this holy fear in us. That is gone today. Nowadays people have no restraints. You need to tell these kids the truth—that suicide is a one-way ticket to hell."

I believe she is right. Sociologist Emile Durkheim said, "Human passions stop only before a moral power that they respect."

The Bible says, "The fear of the Lord is the beginning of wisdom . . ." (Proverbs 9:10). The problem is, this generation has lost its sense of sin and shame, until even

31

suicide is now justified by many. But the Bible is clear about God's ideas concerning suicide.

Is Suicide an Unpardonable Sin?

I told one audience that suicide is a one-way ticket to hell, and a fourteen-year-old girl in the audience began to scream. Later, she told me why. Her mother killed herself about eight years earlier. The girl was angry because of it, and the resentment kept growing. She was determined to commit suicide that very night, but a friend persuaded her to come to my meeting.

"I thought I'd kill myself," she said, "for two reasons. To get even with Mom for what she did. Then, too, maybe I'd be with her in the next world. I hate her, yet I love her."

"But why did you scream when I talked about suicides going to hell?" I asked.

She began to sob. "If my mom is going to hell for killing herself—like you say—I'll never see her again. I don't want to go to hell, either."

I honestly had not tried to scare anyone with hellfire stories, yet I wanted every suicide-prone person to know the unvarnished truth. I had only one answer to give her. I told her how I interpret God's mercy. Those who commit suicide in ignorance of God's laws will be judged according to the light that was in them. To whom little is given, little is expected. But to whom much is given, much is expected.

I said to the girl, "Your mother probably committed suicide without knowing it was sinful. She did it in ignorance of the truth. God is always merciful to those who have never purposely broken His commandments. I can't tell you how God will judge her, but I do know His mercy is great. But for you, it's a different story. You can't do what your mother did—because you know better. You have been told the truth. You now know it is a grievous sin—and you will be judged by the light you have received. So quit thinking of suicide. Don't choose hell."

Thankfully, her life has been turned around. But how many others are there who have never been told the truth about suicide? And even though some ministers don't believe in judgment, and they never use the word *hell*—I can promise you that God's Word makes suicide an unpardonable sin to those who reject His warnings. Once you have read this chapter, you have already heard enough. You can never commit suicide from this day forward, because you have received too much truth on the subject.

Suicidals Commit Seven Deadly Sins

Suicide is a serpent with seven deadly heads. These are the seven sins committed by people who succeed in killing themselves.

A teenager wrote, "Sir, please tell me what the Bible says about suicide. No statistics or psychological stuff—just what the Bible says. Nobody seems to be able to show me why it's so wrong."

Here, then, is exactly what the Bible says about suicide. And God said He honors His Word even above His name.

1. *Suicide is a form of atheism.*

. . . whatsoever is not of faith is sin.

Romans 14:23

We get mad at God. When we need Him the most, He sometimes seems so far away. Our hearts cry out to Him for help, but we feel completely alone and forsaken. We read of all His promises to be there in our times of need—to answer when we call—to give us the desires of our hearts. But the answers don't come on time—our time. Then with David the Psalmist, we cry out,

33

My God, my God, why have you forsaken me? Why are you so far from helping me, and from the words of my roaring? O my God, I cry in the daytime, but you don't hear me; and in the night time I cry out too.

See Psalms 22:1, 2

David said to God, I just don't understand. Others trust in you and they are delivered. Our fathers cried to you and you answered them. Why have others who trusted you received help, but for me there is no help?

See Psalms 22:4–8

In the very next breath David confessed, "I am not a man; I am a worm" (*see* Psalms 22:6).

If Satan can get you to believe God has forsaken you and left you helpless and alone to fight your battles, then he can also make you believe you are a wormlike creature, ready to be trampled. The devil is a sly fox. He wants you to think everybody else is happy and problem free. He wants you to think everybody but you is getting answers to prayer.

I am convinced all suicidal thoughts are incubated in the minds of people who have convinced themselves God has forsaken them and no longer hears their cry for help. So the "abandoned child" is going to get even with God, the absent heavenly Father. "He ran out and left me on my own, so I'll show Him!" They don't say, "God is dead"—just that He is not involved in the affairs of life.

2. *Suicide is satanic seduction!*

Now the Spirit speaketh expressly, that in the latter times some shall depart from the faith, giving heed to seducing spirits . . . having their conscience seared with a hot iron . . . .

1 Timothy 4:1, 2

God has warned us that in these last days of time, some will grow cold in their faith and fall victims to the seductive powers of the devil. Satan is really not as interested in turning you into a drunkard or addict as he is in making you doubt God's promises. He wants you to get mad at God, to hold a grudge against Him.

That grudge against God is destructive. A teenage girl tells me, "How can you expect me to trust God ever again? My mom and dad were both godly ministers—and they were killed in a car crash. How can you believe in a God who takes your parents away from you?"

One fifteen-year-old girl asked, "How can you believe in prayer when it never works for you? I saw my two teenage brothers drown, right before my eyes. I couldn't save them. I prayed they would be rescued, but they died. How can I ever pray again, when God let me down when I really needed Him the most?"

These teenage girls are just two of many who are mad at God today. They feel God failed them in their darkest hour. While others boast about how God answered their prayers, they seemed to get only sorrow and pain. They can't understand why a loving Father would lead them to their destination through a wilderness, rather than by some shortcut. They don't understand that in times of trouble, the deepest works of God are accomplished. He imposes His will in our lives at times, to fulfill a divine purpose beyond our comprehension. Even pain and sorrow can be royal chariots that speed us on our way to true wisdom.

The most difficult thing in this life is to trust God when the lines of communication all seem to be dead; when the heavens seem brass, and there is nothing but silence from above. Don't be angered by that silence. Silence is God's supreme test to prove we trust in His faithfulness.

People who commit suicide die in doubt. They are seduced into living in sin; and sin, when it is finished, brings death. The Bible says, ". . . but the way of the wicked seduceth them . . . . In the way of righteous-

ness is life; and in the pathway thereof there is no death"
(Proverbs 12:26, 28).

3. *Suicide is the sin of hypocrisy!*

Why shall I take my life in my hand? . . . I will trust
. . . because now I know a hypocrite shall not come
before him.

See Job 13:14–16

Job was actually saying, "Why should I do anything
foolish? To take my life in my own hand would make me a
hypocrite—and no hypocrite can stand in God's presence."

Hypocrisy is the sin of putting on false fronts; of faking
it; of pretending. Suicide is like a mountain precipice with
steps one must climb to reach the brink. The last step
before suicide is into a make-believe world of fantasy.
Those who take that final step become confirmed hypocrites.

That hypocrisy includes a smile that covers up a breaking heart. It's phony laughter that camouflages a broken
spirit. It is pretending everything is fine when, in reality,
everything is wrong. Man looks on the outward appear-
ance and can be easily fooled, but God looks on the heart
and sees things as they really are.

A mother wrote me a letter explaining her surprise in
finding a suicide note left by her fourteen-year-old son.
"It shocked me. He was doing so well, I thought. Just
before I found his suicide note, we had a long talk. He
was jovial and never seemed more settled. We didn't
have a single clue that he was wanting to kill himself. He
put up such a good front."

Jesus despised the sin of hypocrisy. He upbraided the
Pharisees, saying, "Woe unto you, scribes and Pharisees,
hypocrites! for ye are like unto whited sepulchres, which
indeed appear beautiful outward, but are within full of
dead men's bones, and of all uncleanness. Even so ye
also outwardly appear righteous unto me, but within ye

are full of hypocrisy and iniquity" (Matthew 23:27, 28).

That is also a concise description of suicidals. They have an outer and an inner shell. They are really two different people. When they die, people are heard to say, "I never really knew him. He never really let anybody know how he felt inside. He kept it all bottled up."

Paul the apostle warned of those who would "speak lies in hypocrisy; having their conscience seared with a hot iron" (*see* 1 Timothy 4:2). When the thought of suicide is "branded" on the mind, as if with a hot branding iron, it results in a shriveled conscience.

People who commit suicide refuse to accept the truth, refuse to tell the truth, and refuse to walk in the truth. Suicide is the ultimate act of hypocrisy. And no hypocrite shall see God.

4. *Suicide is the sin of pride!*

Pride goeth before destruction, and an haughty spirit before a fall.

Proverbs 16:18

Paul warns that people who are "lifted up with pride . . . fall into the condemnation of the devil" (1 Timothy 3:6). Suicide is a fatal fall, brought on by a perverted pride. You see, there are two kinds of pride. Pride actually means "a sense of one's own value and dignity." There is nothing sinful about that kind of pride. It is a pride that says, "God didn't make a mistake when He made me. I'm not here on this earth by accident. God has a plan for me, and I thank Him for making me just what I am."

This good kind of pride rests in the fact we are made in God's image and we should consider that the highest compliment He could give us. "I am one reflection of His many-splendored image—therefore, I have a sense of true dignity." We can be proud of the Christ in us; proud to called the sons of God; proud to be heirs of a kingdom; proud to say, "Make room—a Christian is coming

37

down the street''; proud of His precious promises.

But there is another kind of pride—a perversion of the good kind. Just take God out of the picture, and you have perversion. This corrupted pride, which leads to suicidal destruction, puts man where God should be. You see it everywhere you look today. Perfection can be found in Christ alone, yet thousands struggle to be perfect through their own strength and personal achievements. Our society is perfection-conscious. Everybody strives to be best, to be number one, to be on top, to win the gold medal—second is sinful. And when people can't reach those impossible pride goals, they fall apart.

Harry Bruce was striving for perfection the day he committed suicide. He was only seventeen, a high-school swimming star, and a good musician. His friends called him ''the golden boy,'' because he seemed to be such a success at everything he did.

But Harry was driven by an inner force that made him want to be the best, even perfect. The desire to be perfect became a fatal flaw in his life. It was not enough to be 159th out of a class of 650—he wanted to be in the top ten. He envied other kids who were so ''cool.''

He was popular and fun loving, but he became loud and boisterous to cover up the turmoil in his mind. He tried too hard to be accepted and loved by the crowd.

It happened on a Wednesday. Harry calmly walked to the nearest train station, waited until a locomotive was within several hundred feet, then lay down in front of it, carefully placing his head atop one of the rails. Within minutes, Harry was dead. Ironically, his father worked for the train company.

In a note found in his chemistry book after his death, he apologized for ''messing everything up. School is too hard. Sorry to disappoint you.''

Harry died because he was scared of imperfection; scared to face disapproval of the crowd; fearful of not pleasing his parents; and convinced he was not good enough.

What a terrible tragedy, because if Harry had only known it, probably a majority of all his schoolmates were just as imperfect as he thought he was. All his laughing, carefree friends were nursing hidden fears, too. Many of them were in a state of panic. He just didn't know it. He thought he was the only one afraid.

We get afraid. And the Bible says, "Fear is torment" (*see* Revelation 18:10, 15). It's what we don't know that scares us the most. Everyone has his own kind of fear.

5. *Suicide is the sin of lying!*

> These six things doth the Lord hate: yea, seven are an abomination unto him: A proud look, a lying tongue, and hands that shed innocent blood, An heart that deviseth wicked imaginations, feet that be swift in running to mischief, A false witness that speaketh lies, and he that soweth discord among brethren.
>
> Proverbs 6:16–19

Suicide is the biggest lie of all. It is a person's way of proclaiming to the world, "God put me here by mistake. My life is in vain. It has no purpose to it—so I'll end it."

That makes God out a liar, also. Those who kill themselves are in actuality saying, "God made a fool of me—putting me here just to tease and taunt me. I'm just an accident. If He really had a plan or purpose for me, He would never have allowed my life to get so messed up. God ought to get pleasure out of my death."

But God says, "Have I any pleasure at all that the wicked should die? saith the Lord God: and not that he should return from his ways, and live?" (Ezekiel 18:23).

The truth is, God never afflicts or grieves a child of His willingly. And Christ is always standing before the heavenly Father, pleading our case, knowing God is love. The Bible says,

> For he doth not afflict willingly nor grieve the children of men. To crush under his feet all the prisoners

of the earth, To turn aside the right of a man . . . To subvert a man in his cause, the Lord approveth not.

Lamentations 3:33–36

Suicide is man's way of protesting to God, "You never gave me a chance. You turned Your head when I asked for my rights. You ruined my plans. You ran over me with some master plan I knew nothing about. It's unfair." And that is all a big lie.

Suicide is an illustrated, visual lie one tells against God. When that lifeless body is laid out in a casket for the world to see, it is a lying statement that says, "Here is an example of God's unfaithfulness. Here lies a body that witnesses to an unreachable God. Here are the abandoned bones of one who can say the Bible doesn't work. Here is the corpse of one whose God wouldn't help in time of need. Here lies one of God's failures."

I am convinced when suicidals stand before the judgment seat of Christ, He will ask them, "Why did you make God out as such a liar? Why did you allow your death to disgrace the love of God?"

There can be no getting around the bluntness of God's threat to liars, ". . . and all liars, shall have their part in the lake which burneth with fire and brimstone: which is the second death" (Revelation 21:8).

6. *Suicide is an attack on the body of Christ!*

So we, being many, are one body in Christ, and every one members one of another.

Romans 12:5

Know ye not that your bodies are the members of Christ? . . .

1 Corinthians 6:15

For as the body is one, and hath many members . . . But now are they many members, yet but one body . . . And whether one member suffer, all

40

the members suffer with it . . . Now ye are the body of Christ, and members in particular.

1 Corinthians 12:12, 20, 26, 27

For we are members of his body, of his flesh, and of his bones.

Ephesians 5:30

For none of us liveth to himself, and no man dieth to himself.

Romans 14:7

It is impossible for a believer to commit suicide without wounding the body of Christ. Suicide is not an isolated, single act of destruction. Never! We are all joined in the Lord, members of His flesh and of His bones. And when one member of that body suffers, the whole body feels pain.

Suicide is an act of mutilation on the body of Christ. It is an effort to amputate oneself from the rest of the body. Would anyone dare to walk into the throne room of Christ and amputate one of His fingers? Would anyone dare march into His presence with a deadly weapon and cut off an arm or leg, causing Him to suffer and bleed?

As gruesome as it may sound, that is exactly what suicide means. It means an attack on the body of Christ. "For we are members of his body, of his flesh, and of his bones" (Ephesians 5:30). Suicide is an assault with a deadly weapon against the very Son of God! And there is no way to get around that fact.

Suicide is more than an act of self-destruction. It is an act of violence against the entire church of Jesus Christ. I know most suicidals convince themselves they are no longer worthy to be considered a part of that body. But Jesus doesn't abandon believers just because they are depressed and confused. It is tragic so many faithless Christians destroy themselves without realizing the suffering it causes others.

41

When a person commits suicide, the rest of the body bleeds. The dead victim only wanted to destroy himself—to get out of the way of others. But instead, the victim leaves behind a mutilated body agonizing in pain. Family, friends, and loved ones are left to bleed and suffer.

Some do commit suicide to make others suffer. But, oh, how selfish and cowardly that is. It's like double murder. The victim not only kills himself, he leaves behind another victim, who often dies a little bit every day because of regrets and memories.

God help the person who must stand before Christ on the day of Judgment to answer for an assault against His body. What a horrible moment when Christ, the Judge, must point to a mighty host of redeemed believers and say, "You hurt every one of them. You wounded My body. You did not live or die to yourself. We all suffered by what you did."

> For none of us liveth to himself, and no man dieth to himself.
>
> Romans 14:7

7. *Suicide is blasphemy against the Holy Ghost!*

> . . . the blasphemy against the Holy Ghost shall not be forgiven unto men . . . it shall not be forgiven him, neither in this world, neither in the world to come.
>
> Matthew 12:31, 32

The Bible says our body is the temple of the Holy Ghost. To destroy that temple is to blaspheme. It is an unpardonable sin to those who act against truth.

The Pharisees of Christ's time committed the unpardonable sin in their minds. Blasphemy against the Holy Ghost has to do with thoughts. The Pharisees witnessed Christ's miracles. They saw Christ make the dumb speak

42

and the blind see. They had talked with people Christ raised from the dead. They knew in their hearts He was the divine Son of God. They knew He had all power. Yet, they closed their minds to Him and refused to believe God was with Him. "And Jesus knew their thoughts . . ." (Matthew 12:25).

Jesus, in describing the unpardonable sin, said, "I can forgive your words against me as a person—but when you deny the Holy Spirit in me—that can never be forgiven" (*see* Matthew 12:31, 32).

The work of the Holy Ghost is to bring us to Christ; to comfort and guide us through the trials of life; to minister to us when we are down; to make a way when there seems to be none; to show us truth, so we will not be tossed about by the lies of the enemy. He, the Holy Ghost, is to be in us a well of refreshing water that springs up to heal our wounds. He is the one who takes the words of Jesus and makes them come alive to us.

Suicide hinders the Holy Ghost from doing His work. To kill oneself is to blaspheme the Holy Ghost by destroying His habitation and denying His right to work. Suicide is "speaking against the Holy Ghost" in a most certain way. It is an act of violence that says to the world, "The Holy Ghost is an apparition. He does not exist. He did nothing for me. He did not comfort or guide me. All that is said about His power is false. The Holy Ghost is a lie."

Suicide not only makes the Holy Ghost out as a liar, it denies His divine power. It mocks His reality. It attributes more power to Satan than the Spirit. And that, my friend, is a sin God will never forgive—not in this world or in eternity.

Even more important, suicide robs God of praise that belongs to Him. We have been put on this earth to praise Him. Suicide silences a vessel destined to praise and worship God. King Hezekiah wanted to live to fulfill that purpose. He said, "For the grave cannot praise thee, death cannot celebrate thee: they that go down into the pit cannot hope for thy truth. The living, the living . . . shall praise thee . . ." (Isaiah 38:18, 19). To destroy a temple of God made for the purpose of praise is unpardonable.

These seven sins of suicide are but a few of many mentioned in the Bible. But perhaps the most important command against suicide in all God's Word is the sixth commandment, "Thou shalt not kill" (Exodus 20:13). Not another, nor yourself.

4

Giving Up

There comes a critical moment in nearly everyone's life when death seems to be the only escape. One expert in the field claims that more than 80 percent of the population admits to having "played" with suicidal ideas. I know for a fact multitudes of young people now entertain thoughts of suicide, and the number grows daily.

Even Christians Flirt With Suicidal Thoughts

Even the most devoted Christian can reach such a low point in life, all hope seems to be gone. Everything goes wrong. One bad experience follows another. Troubles pile up. Prayers that were prayed in simple faith seem to go unanswered. The joy that is supposed to follow weeping doesn't come. The problems of others press in, with no solutions in sight. Wave after wave of fear and despair come on, like an overwhelming tide. Depression strikes and nothing seems to shake it loose. Sickness and pain begin to wear down faith and trust in God. The future looks dark and uncertain. Satan whispers, "Nothing works. Faith in God doesn't produce results. In spite of all your tears, prayers, and trust in God's Word—nothing changes. Days, weeks, and even years roll by, and your prayers, hopes, and dreams are still unanswered and unfulfilled. Quit! Give up!"

Every human on earth reaches that crisis point at one time or another in life. And in that moment, when the walls seem to be pressing in and the roof appears to be falling, when things look like they are coming apart—a voice deep inside cries out, "Walk away from it. Just pack it all in and escape. Don't take it for another minute.

Do something drastic." But you usually don't—because you have no place to go, and you still have the fear of God in you.

David Went to the Brink

There are a number of famous Bible characters who flirted with ideas of suicide. David is perhaps the most noted of all. This great man of God descended so low and became so depressed, he could think only of hastening his escape (*see* Psalms 55:8). Listen to the language of a man on the brink:

There is no rest in my bones because of my sin.
See Psalms 38:3

I am troubled . . . bowed down . . . mourning all the day long . . . there is no relief . . . .
See v. 6

There is a roaring inside . . . light is gone out . . . my strength faileth . . . .
See vv. 8, 10

. . . the terrors of death are fallen upon me. Fearfulness and trembling are come upon me, and horror hath overwhelmed me.
Psalms 55:4, 5

To make things worse, David was forsaken and deeply hurt by friends and family. He said,

They that hate me . . . are more than the hairs of mine head . . . I am become a stranger unto my brethren . . . .
Psalms 69:4, 8

"God Has Let Me Down"

David even thought God had forsaken him. He considered his loneliness, his deep hurts, his inner longings, and he began to see himself as one sinking in mud and drowning in waters of terror. He cried: "I sink in deep mire, where there is no standing . . . the floods overflow me" (Psalms 69:2). ". . . lighten mine eyes, lest I sleep the sleep of death" (Psalms 13:3).

This man God so loved began to question his heavenly Father's concern for him. Overwhelmed by feelings of being forsaken, he prayed aloud, "Awake, why do you sleep? Cast me not off . . . why do you hide? Why do you forget?" (see Psalms 44:23, 24).

He reminded God of his sad condition. Describing himself as "half dead," he identified with people who had lost their will to live. He said, "I am counted with them that go down into the pit . . ." (Psalms 88:4). ". . . my life draweth nigh unto the grave . . . Free among the dead, like the slain that lie in the grave, whom thou rememberest no more . . . cut off . . ." (Psalms 88:3, 5).

He talked of "walking through the valley of the shadow of death." His appetite was gone. He said, "I forget to eat" (see Psalms 102:4). He became so bitter, he prayed for revenge on everyone who had hurt him. "Pour out thine indignation upon them, and let thy wrathful anger take hold of them" (Psalms 69:24).

"I Am Worthless—No Good!"

David hit bottom. And it was then he lost all confidence in himself. He began to put himself down, to see himself as nothing but a shadow of his old self. A pitiful self-image emerged. He saw himself now as worthless, with nothing left but to wither away into nothingness. That's right! This great man of God, who killed giants, led massive armies to victory, pulled the limbs of lions and bears apart—now referred to himself as a lonely little bird, just

47

wasting away. Listen to his confession, "I am like a little sparrow . . . sitting all alone upon the house tops . . . my days are like declining shadows . . . I am withering like grass . . ." (*see* Psalms 102:7, 11).

This great warrior, who once stood self-confident in a string of successes and victories, now sought only pity. He cared nothing now for the praise and adulation of the crowd. He wanted to hear no more of their songs extolling his heroic exploits. He had no strength left in him to help and comfort others. No more would he protect the rights of others and allow them to lean on him.

David was now the one needing help and comfort. He was weak and felt all alone. He had come to the end of himself, and the only goal left in his life was to find a little comfort and pity. ". . . I looked for some to take pity, but there was none; and for comforters, but I found none" (Psalms 69:20).

A Way Out

David overcame his death wish by getting out of himself and into God's precious promises. He awoke one day and said to himself—"That is enough. Why be cast down, O my soul . . . He is the health of my countenance . . . God will redeem my soul from the power of the grave . . . I am going to walk in the light of the living" (*see* Psalms 43:5; 49:15; 56:13).

He began to seek God as "the fountain of life," but he realized this life-giving water had to be drawn from the well of his own free will. In other words, God can lead you to the water, but He can't force you to drink. That well of life-giving water is inside us all. Faith alone can cause it to "spring up" and water the soul and wash away every evil death wish.

Jonah Thought of Suicide

Jonah, too, was overcome by a sudden death wish. In a desperate act of self-preservation, this prophet ran from responsibility and ended up in the belly of a whale. Finally, he did go to the wicked city of Nineveh to warn them of impending destruction if they refused to repent. "God will wipe your city off the map unless you repent now!" he cried (*see* Jonah 3:4). And they did repent.

But, rather than rejoice in their heeding his message, Jonah sat on a hill overlooking the city, waiting for God to make him look good. He was a prophet sent by God, and he wanted his prophecies to be accurate. He did not want to come out looking like a liar.

God spared Nineveh. Jonah was offended. He saw himself only as a failure. "What will people say now? I'm out on a limb, and now it's been cut out from under me. My word is worthless. I'm a complete failure." A death wish flashed through his mind. Obsessed by his self-pity and sense of failure, he prayed: ". . . O Lord, take, I beseech thee, my life from me; for it is better for me to die than to live" (Jonah 4:3).

"I'm Better Off Dead Than Alive"

What a familiar sound. "I'm better off dead than alive." Like Jonah, even modern-day Christians can fall into the same trap of Satan. It is possible to tell the whole world about things God has promised to do for and through you. You can testify how the Lord has healed you and how He is going to use and guide you.

Then it appears to blow up in your face. The pain and symptoms return. What you said would happen, doesn't happen. Everything changes. God leads you down an entirely new path. You change course in the middle of the stream. You sound like a liar. You appear to be deceived. Like Jonah, you are then tempted into believing you have failed—failed to hear from God properly. You feel self-deceived and are left smashed and defeated. What you have testified to and preached about appears to blow up in your face. You think to yourself, "How could I have been so wrong? I was only doing what I thought was right. I meant well. I really thought God had led me. But I

49

guess it was just an invention of my own mind. I've failed somewhere. I don't know how to hear from God."

"A Loss of Face"

This loss-of-face syndrome caused the suicidal death of Ahithophel, a former counselor to King Absalom. When the king rejected his counsel for the advice of one of his political contemporaries, Ahithophel's world caved in. He overheard King Absalom say, "The counsel of Hushai is better than the counsel of Ahithophel" (*see* 2 Samuel 17:14).

He saw his influence vanishing before his eyes. He said to himself, "I'm all washed up. I'm a has-been. Nobody listens to me anymore. I'm a total failure. What good is it to live if nobody takes you seriously? I got pushed right out of the picture. It's not fair!"

The loss of honor and dignity can be devastating, as can the loss of an important job. Having known what it means to be wanted and needed, then suddenly "put on the shelf," out of sight, can be demoralizing. Ahithophel was once chief counsel to the mighty King David. He received ambassadors from many nations. He was there when war plans were conceived. He had the king's ear. His job was vital to the nation's security. But now, bright young men moved in and pushed him out. He was a liability; just kept around because people felt sorry for him.

King David must have feared this loss of face, also. He prayed, "Cast me not off in the time of old age; forsake me not when my strength faileth . . . when I am old and greyheaded . . ." (Psalms 71:9, 18).

It is so despairing to feel unnecessary—to look in the mirror one day and say, "Nobody really needs me anymore. I'm good to no one now. I'm just a burden. People just feel sorry for me. I get no respect. I might as well be dead—no one would care."

What a pitiful ending to a great career as adviser to kings. Fear, depression, and a feeling of having lost face led to Ahithophel's suicide.

And when Ahithophel saw that his counsel was not
followed, he saddled his ass, and arose, and gat him
home to his house, to his city, and put his household
in order, and hanged himself, and died . . . .

2 Samuel 17:23

Judas Committed Suicide

Judas committed suicide because he thought his sin
was so bad it could never be forgiven. He betrayed the
Son of God, and his traitorous sin brought him to despair.
Condemnation overwhelmed him. He cried out, "I have
sinned. I have betrayed innocent blood." He acknowl-
edged his sin, and the Bible says he "repented himself."

Then Judas, which had betrayed him, when he saw
that he was condemned, repented himself, and
brought again the thirty pieces of silver . . . Saying,
I have sinned in that I have betrayed innocent
blood . . . And he cast down the pieces of silver in
the temple, and departed, and went and hanged himself.

Matthew 27:3–5

"I Can't Be Forgiven"

Judas committed suicide by hanging himself because
he could not bring himself to believe Jesus could ever
forgive him. So it is today. Thousands of people today
face the "Judas dilemma." Knowing they have sinned
grievously—having trampled the blood of Christ
underfoot—having crucified Him afresh and put Him to
open shame—having been a traitor to His love—they refuse to accept the Lord's forgiveness. Jesus forgives all
confessed sin, no matter how exceedingly wicked or
abominable. But what He offers must be accepted. Only
God knows how many people have destroyed themselves
because they convinced themselves they were "just like
Judas"—a traitorous, unforgiven, hopeless failure—
deserving to die!

51

5

Spoon Suicide

Eli was a judge in Israel whose death was recorded as accidental. He died from a broken neck suffered in a fall. Yet, upon closer examination, it could be said Eli died from "spoon suicide." He was fat!

This man had two delinquent sons, who assisted him in the ministry. They committed fornication with women; they lived reckless lives of compromise. During the sacrifice, the priests were permitted to use fleshhooks to pull out of the boiling pots meat for their own tables. It was their portion, ordained by God.

But Hophni and Phinehas hated boiled meat. They preferred prime cuts off the hoof rather than the sodden flesh of the pots. When worshippers brought their sacrifice to the temple, these two sons would cut out the fillets for themselves. Evidently Eli had developed a taste for this prime meat being smuggled into the priests' quarters. The Bible says, ". . . he restrained them not" (1 Samuel 3:13).

> They took as much as their soul desired.
>
> *See* 1 Samuel 2:16

This materialistic, easy-living addiction took its toll. Eli became a soft judge, unable to control his sons' or his own ravenous appetite.

He was ninety-eight years old on that fateful day. He was sitting by the side of the road in Shiloh waiting for dispatches from the war zone. The Philistine army had smitten the forces of Israel and 30,000 infantrymen were slaughtered. The rest of the army was in disarray. Worse, the ark of God was captured, and Eli's two sons were killed in the battle.

A Benjamite messenger escaped and ran to tell Eli the

bad news. ". . . Israel is fled before the Philistines, and there hath been also a great slaughter among the people, and thy two sons also, Hophni and Phinehas, are dead, and the ark of God is taken" (1 Samuel 4:17).

Eli was stunned. His heart began to flutter, for he ". . . trembled for the ark of God . . ." (1 Samuel 4:13). "And it came to pass, when he made mention of the ark of God, that he fell from off the seat backward by the side of the gate, and his neck brake, and he died: for he was an old man, and heavy . . ." (1 Samuel 4:18).

He fell backward, broke his neck, and died. How? Because he was old? Yes, partly. But the Bible says he was heavy. Usually, elderly people who fall off chairs do not die. I am sure the tragic news and his age contributed to his death. But he died partly because he was heavy.

I am sure there are people today who are committing spoon suicide just like Eli did. They would never slit a wrist or swallow an overdose of pills. But the same forces that drive people to take their lives suddenly, cause other people to take their lives slowly. Not with a gun, just a spoon.

They get discouraged—so they eat. Everything goes wrong—so they eat. The beautiful things they long for and pray for don't seem to come their way—so they eat. They can't find love—so they eat. Something that seems so sure, within their grasp, blows up in their face—so they eat. A powerful force within drives them to consume food. They devour it with a passion. It's as real an addiction as drugs, alcohol, or tobacco.

In such hands, a spoon becomes a fatal weapon. All kinds of inner needs blend into one overwhelming craving for food! It often ends in death by "caloric overdose."

I'll never forget the pitifully overweight teenage girl who asked me to help her overcome a nagging suicide wish. She was obese—so overweight, she could hardly walk. "Look at me," she said, "I'm fat and ugly. Other kids laugh at me and call me names. But deep inside me, there is a girl just like everybody else. I have the same néeds and desires all the attractive girls have. I'm not a freak. I don't want to be like this. I want to be free from all this fat. But nothing I do works. I feel doomed for the rest of my life. That's why I keep thinking of suicide. At least that's one way to stop the agony.''

I wanted to cry. Mostly because I meet so many like her today, everywhere I go. They are terribly overweight, and consequently, they despise themselves. You've heard it said, ''Fat people are jolly.'' Don't believe it! Deep within, they know there is another personality—a new body—free from fat. The jolliness is just a cover-up. Overweight people do get hurt by all the wisecracking, the whispers behind their backs, the rejection heaped upon them. Too often that hurt is so deep, it leads to suicide.

The overweight teenager admitted to me she was totally undisciplined in her eating habits. She snacked constantly. She claimed to have tried dieting, but because she couldn't lose weight fast enough, she'd get discouraged and eat all the more. It was a vicious cycle. Like Eli, the judge of Israel, she lacked restraint. Restraint is ''an act of holding back.''

No one today needs to be obese. Glands have very little to do with it. That is just an alibi to cover up the real problem. The problem is an overdose of food. It is caused by an undisciplined appetite. It is slow death, suicide on the installment plan—no matter how you try to explain it.

The solution? Get angry at yourself. God said to David, ''Get hold on yourself.'' To Job, God said, ''Gird yourself. Prepare to change.'' To all overweight people the message is, ''Quit crying. Wake up and get to it! Restrain yourself. Go 'cold turkey' on food—withdraw! Begin right now—not sometime later. Why kill yourself?''

You don't need a miracle. Prayer is not what you need, either. You need indignation against your foolish habits—a holy anger against bondage to food. Your whole outlook on life will change—friends will respect you—and the discipline will affect every other area of your life.

6

Sudden Suicide

Be not afraid of sudden fear . . . . For the Lord shall be thy confidence, and shall keep thy foot from being taken.

Proverbs 3:25, 26

The thought of suicide can strike suddenly. Well-balanced people, who have never once entertained such thoughts, can find themselves in a crisis that ends in a suicide attempt. It happened to the Philippian jailer.

Paul and Silas were two troublesome itinerant evangelists who came to Philippi from the city of Neapolis. It seems their preaching had upset the entire city. They cast demons out of a well-known fortune-teller. The Mafia-type element in that city was incensed, because she fronted for them in a very profitable psychic racket.

The two Roman preachers were dragged before the magistrate and charged with inciting violence. After beating them with many lashes, they cast them into prison. The jailer was taken aside and given explicit instructions to place them in maximum security. So the jailer, "having received such a charge," placed them in the inner cell block and locked their feet in a stockade (see Acts 16:24).

As was their custom, Paul and Silas prayed and sang aloud when in a crisis. The entire jail listened, probably in amazement, as these two strange ministers sang and prayed until midnight. Meanwhile, the jail keeper fell asleep.

Suddenly there was an earthquake! The very foundations of that prison were shaken. And immediately all the cell doors flung open, and all the chains and stockades were ripped from the walls.

The jailer was awakened. To his horror, it was "open house" at his jail. All he could see were open gates, open cell bars—but no one in sight. Observe now how quickly a person can contemplate suicide. In one Bible verse, we have a lesson on suicide that is one of the most important in all the Bible.

> And the keeper of the prison awakening out of his sleep, and seeing the prison doors open, he drew out his sword, and would have killed himself, supposing that the prisoners had been fled.

> Acts 16:27

Listening to Lies

He had not been brooding for months. He was not a depressive maniac. Suicide was the furthest thing from his mind when he locked Paul and Silas up and then decided to take a little nap. A man thinking of suicide could not have slept through all the praying and singing of those two loud evangelists.

But suddenly he was in the middle of a crisis. The jail was in a shambles, the doors were all open, the locks all split apart. He slept through it all. His imagination ran wild. No doubt he imagined his prisoners roaming freely about the city of Philippi, robbing, breaking into houses, mugging pedestrians. "And those two evangelists are probably halfway to Macedonia by now," so he must have thought.

He was a failure! He could see no way out. How could he explain the chaos, the loose prisoners, the empty prison? How could he face his family, his bosses? How could he ever walk the streets again as a respected man? He would be the laughingstock of the city. "The fool jailer who slept through the biggest jailbreak ever, with everybody escaping."

Fear is dangerous. A wild imagination can conjure up

58

all kinds of hopeless dilemmas. Thinking all the prisoners were gone, he raised the sword, no doubt ready to plunge it into his heart.

Think of it—he almost killed himself for nothing. Suppose that sword pierced his heart. He falls to the strewn floor, dying. Hearing his groans, Paul and Silas and the rest of the prisoners gather around him. Their cell doors were open, their chains unshackled—but they were all still there. Can you picture Paul leaning over this man to pray, and asking, "Why, Sir, did you do such a terrible thing? Why did you try to kill yourself? Why suicide?"

"Because," the jailer would have to answer, "I thought you were all gone. There was no other way out. I saw my world coming to an end. I had failed."

But Paul, seeing him about to commit suicide, cried out with a loud voice, "Do yourself no harm; we are all still here" (see Acts 16:28). In other words, "Don't commit suicide! It's not the way you think. You are not a failure. Your mind is playing tricks on you. Don't believe what you see. Hold still—everything's going to be all right."

God's Simple Solution

How quickly God's Word dispels the fog and gets right to the point. In two simple verses, the Bible reveals how to win over suicidal thoughts.

Then he called for a light, and sprang in, and came trembling, and fell down before Paul and Silas . . . and said, Sirs, what must I do to be saved?
                                                    Acts 16:29, 30

There you have it. Reach for your Bible—throw down your pills—and fall on your knees before the Lord and repent! Too much of a simplistic answer? Just whitewashing the real problems? No! This man had nearly killed himself. He wanted some lifesaving answers, quickly. So, he did what every person on this earth must do—

without exception—to be set free from sudden attempts at suicide. Go to the source of truth, because only truth sets men free. Get into the Bible—find your answers there. Humble yourself! Repent and "believe on the Lord Jesus, and you shall be saved" (*see* Acts 16:31). Saved from sin—saved from suicide.

The jailer was converted to Christ. His entire family was unified behind him. Defeat and failure were turned into a new life, better than before. God will do the same for every repentant person today. His promise to you is, "Thou shalt be saved, *and* thy house" (*see* Acts 16:31).

7

Double Suicide

Then said Saul unto his armourbearer, Draw thy sword, and thrust me through therewith . . . But his armourbearer would not . . . Therefore Saul took a sword, and fell upon it. And when his armourbearer saw that Saul was dead, he fell likewise upon his sword, and died with him.

1 Samuel 31:4, 5

King Saul lay dying on mount Gilboa, wounded by an archer's arrow. His army had defected, having been soundly defeated by the Philistines. His three sons—Jonathan, Abinadab, and Melchishua—were killed in the battle.

This proud king and his armourbearer were surrounded by enemy troops who were ready to take him prisoner and publicly abuse him. He was to be their victory trophy. Saul knew well enough what that would mean. He would be dragged through enemy streets, spat upon, tortured, and murdered, and his head hung from an idol temple.

"Get your sword and kill me," Saul commanded of his servant. "I'll not be taken alive by those uncircumcised Philistines. Save me from torture." He was seriously wounded and unable to run. But the armourbearer was afraid to inflict a mercy killing on the king.

Saul committed suicide! He thrust a sword through his body and died. But before night fell on mount Gilboa, two men would be dead from suicide. The armourbearer killed himself, also.

An elderly minister is told he has terminal cancer. He decides to "die with dignity," and he takes an overdose of pills. Confiding his plans in his wife, she said, "Honey, I don't want to live without you. I'm going, too. We'll do it together." They made a double-suicide pact.

A few days later, their son found them in the bedroom, both dead from an overdose of pills. A note left on an open Bible read, "We hope God and our children will forgive us. We didn't want to be a burden on anyone. We were going to die soon, anyway. Forgive us. Good-bye."

They were eulogized by some who said, "Wasn't that a romantic thing to do? Weren't they brave? God understands. Cancer would have taken him soon, anyway."

How tragic. Because God is not pleased with those who take the key of life and death in their own hands. We cannot play God. We dare not abuse this temple of God—our flesh.

A growing number of teenage lovers are committing suicide in doubles. They love each other deeply, but their parents want them to break up. Like Saul, they feel "sorely wounded" and see no way out of their dilemma. They decide to leave the world together, secretly hoping they will spend eternity as lovers.

Was Saul justified in committing suicide? Wasn't his situation hopeless? Isn't that better than torture and extended periods of pain and agony? What's wrong with terminally ill people choosing to die rather than to live in pain and fear of a long, debilitating illness? What could be sinful about two people who want to die while they are still together, rather than be separated by a tragedy? Why not pull the plug and let comatose invalids die? Who is the judge?

> For to him that is joined to all the living there is hope: for a living dog is better than a dead lion.
>
> Ecclesiastes 9:4

Actually, suicide never solves anything. Saul was still beheaded by enemy forces who found his body. His head and body were hung on the wall of Bethshan, an enemy city. Family and friends were left to suffer the consequences. They slipped into Bethshan in the middle of the night, and at the risk of their lives, took the bodies of Saul and his three sons off the wall and buried them under a tree in Jabesh-gilead.

Saul did not have to commit suicide. Nor did his servant. God could have healed him. David and his troops were already returning from slaughtering the Amalekites, and he would have surely marched into the Philistine camp and delivered the king and his servant. There is every evidence he could have survived. He also begged a passing Amalekite to kill him, saying, ". . . slay me: for anguish is come upon me, because my life is yet whole in me" (2 Samuel 1:9).

No situation is hopeless when God is on His throne. There is no such thing as "terminal" with God, because all things are possible with Him. Thousands of "terminal" cases have been miraculously healed. Suicide robs God of ever getting glory from such miracles. Until the last breath in the body, there is hope. Suicide annihilates hope. That makes it a spiritual as well as a physical disaster.

He that is our God is the God of salvation; and unto God the Lord belong the issues from death.
Psalms 68:20

63

8

Job's Fatal Urge

The Book of Job is a story about a man of God who overcame an urge to die. He was a man who lost everything. All his children died in tragedies. He went from great riches to abject poverty. His wife and friends suggested he curse God and take his life. The terror and agony of this troubled man brought him to the edge of the grave. His battle with the death urge and his ultimate victory over despair is a story of hope for those who have been afflicted with that same, fatal urge.

Let's get into the life of Job and discover secrets about overcoming suicide that are unknown to modern sciences and therapies. These secrets are revealed only in God's Holy Word. This is the only truth that really sets man free from thoughts of suicide.

Job Lost Hope

Job's first thought of death came upon him when his days were spent without hope (*see* Job 7:6). Without hope, he could no longer sleep. ". . . I am full of tossings to and fro unto the dawning of the day" (Job 7:4).

His nights were haunted by visions and scary dreams. He began to hate new mornings, and even light of day could not chase away his sorrow. "For the morning is . . . even as the shadow of death . . ." (Job 24:17).

Thoughts of suicide began to plague his mind. He said to those around him, "Ye shall see me no more . . . ye shall seek me in the morning, but I shall not be . . ." (*see* Job 7:8, 21). Once committed to that thought, the urge grew stronger. He thought of what would happen to him with resignation. "The graves are ready for me" (Job 17:1).

Destined to Die

Job began to think of himself as "an appointed victim." He viewed other people as happy, carefree, and untouched by the kind of problems that afflicted him. While other people would die happy and peaceful, he would die with bitterness of soul, because he was one of those victims destined to fade under a cloud of grief.

"Some die full of strength . . . happy . . . at ease . . . others, like me . . . die in bitterness of soul . . ." (*see* Job 21:23–25). The grave became his goal. He said, "The grave is my house. I am going to make my bed in hell" (*see* Job 17:13). He began to speak like a man already dead, with "days already past . . . purposes already broken off . . ." (*see* Job 17:11).

Now, he was longing for death. Like a magnet, he was beginning to feel drawn to it. He cried out in despair, "I wish to die . . . to be cut off." And why this wish to die? Because he was "hardened in sorrow" (*see* Job 6:10). "My heart is too hard to feel anything good about life." He spoke of "longing for death . . . digging for it . . . bitter in soul . . ." (*see* Job 3:20, 21).

The Seeds of Suicide

What kind of overwhelming influence brings a person to the brink of death? What drives a person so low that he wants to die—yes, and to even look forward to it? Why does a normal person who loves God even flirt with such fatal urges? What goes wrong? How and why do thoughts of suicide begin? What brings a person to say, as Job did, "Let me alone . . . my days are worthless . . . I am a burden to myself . . ." (*see* Job 7:16, 20). Why do intelligent human beings so despair of life they seek ". . . the land of darkness and the shadow of death . . . without any order . . ." (Job 10:21, 22)?

Job listed six reasons for loathing life to the point of quitting. Every completed suicide since the beginning of time can be traced to at least one or more of these reasons. All the real causes are here, in one form or another.

1. *A feeling of being forsaken by God.* Job began to think God had abandoned him. God was "in hiding." He could no longer communicate with the heavenly Father to plead his cause. He cried, "Oh that I knew where I might find him! that I might come even to his seat! I would order my cause before him, and fill my mouth with arguments" (Job 23:3, 4).

Job's agony came from a terrible dilemma. He was convinced in his heart God knew where he was and what he was going through. Yet, he himself could not enter into the presence of God. "Behold," said Job, "I go forward, but he is not there; and backward, but I cannot perceive him: On the left hand, where he doth work, but I cannot behold him; he hideth himself on the right hand, that I cannot see him" (Job 23:8, 9).

Job was saying to himself, "I know God is there someplace, looking down on me in all my trouble. He knows the way I take—but in spite of all I do to find Him, He keeps hiding from me. I believe God is real, He is there, but I just can't see Him." In total desperation, Job sobs, ". . . I am afraid of him . . . the Almighty troubleth me" (Job 23:15, 16). And all those fearful and troubled thoughts about God were the result of what Job thought was a divine do-nothingness. Job argues, "You don't cut me off, yet you don't remove the darkness" (*see* Job 23:17). The bottom line for Job was simply this: Either cut me down or make things right—just don't be silent toward me! Even if You cut me off, at least I'll know You are there.

2. *God no longer answers prayer. You are left to work things out for yourself!* It follows that if God is hiding, He has shut His ears to all prayers. The Bible says, ". . . the sorrow of the world worketh death" (2 Corinthians 7:10).

Job's sorrow was working certain death in him. He

cried and wept in prayer. "My face," he said, "is foul with weeping, and on my eyelids is the shadow of death" (Job 16:16). But, ". . . my prayer is pure" (Job 16:17). He was sure he was praying the best he knew how.

Job pictured himself as a doomed prisoner, whose prayers were like supplication to a judge (*see* Job 9:15). But he was being afflicted and wounded without cause. Why seek forgiveness when he had not sinned? Why call on God when there are no answers? Job was sure God would not listen to his prayers. "If I had called, and he had answered me; yet would I not believe that he had hearkened unto my voice" (Job 9:16).

Why wouldn't Job believe God heard him? Because, in spite of all his calling and praying and weeping, ". . . he breaketh me with a tempest, and multiplieth my wounds . . ." (Job 9:17).

Job was saying, "If God answers prayer, why hasn't anything changed? I'm still afraid. Things keep going from bad to worse. My life is still stormy and upset." And Job thought that was cruel of God. "Thou art become cruel to me: with thy strong hand thou opposest thyself against me" (Job 30:21).

Listen to Job's lament: ". . . I waited for light, there came darkness" (Job 30:26). "I cry unto thee, and thou dost not hear me . . ." (Job 30:20). "Behold, I cry out of wrong, but I am not heard: I cry aloud, but there is no judgment" (Job 19:7). Having convinced himself that God was not hearing or answering his prayers, Job lost all sense of direction. God was no longer involved in his daily life. God was not leading, guiding, or directing his footsteps. God just puts you on this earth, then lets you blow about in the wind. You are swept about by hurricane forces. "Thou liftest me up to the wind; thou causest me to ride upon it, and dissolvest my substance" (Job 30:22).

3. *God was unfair to pick on him!* Not only had God forsaken Job; no longer was God not answering his prayers; to make matters worse, God had it in for him.

God was picking on him. It was unfair. "God is hurting me so much, He acts like I'm His enemy instead of a friend," thought Job.

> He hath fenced up my way that I cannot pass, and he hath set darkness in my paths. He hath stripped me of my glory, and taken the crown from my head. He hath destroyed me on every side, and I am gone . . . He hath also kindled his wrath against me, and he counteth me unto him as one of his enemies.
>
> Job 19:8–11

Job saw himself as God's whipping boy. God was always spanking him. He pouted, "Let him take his rod away from me, and let not his fear terrify me" (Job 9:34). "Oh, God," he cried, "You have poured me out as milk, and curdled me like cheese" (*see* Job 10:10).

Job wanted to know what God had against him. Why was he being picked on so much? ". . . shew me wherefore thou contendest with me" (Job 10:2).

He couldn't understand what was happening to him at all. One day he was minding his own business, at peace with himself and the world, and suddenly trouble breaks in on him. Now, he was a marked man, being shaken to pieces by God. Job thought God hated him. So much so, God had him by the neck, choking him. God was not only against him, God had turned him over to wicked forces.

> God hath delivered me to the ungodly, and turned me over into the hands of the wicked. I was at ease, but he hath broken me asunder: he hath also taken me by my neck, and shaken me to pieces, and set me up for his mark.
>
> Job 16:11, 12

This, my friend, is the seed of all suicide. The feeling that God has set you up as a mark, to live in depression

69

and sorrow; that God is somehow mad at you and is shaking you to pieces to make you pay; and that God has given up on you, leaving you to the powers of the devil.

4. *An inability to understand himself*. Mankind has always been preoccupied with trying to "understand oneself." It is a burden too heavy to bear. Life cannot be enjoyed, because so much time is consumed in trying to answer the questions, "Who am I? Why am I here? What's life all about?"

Job saw life passing by without him perceiving the meaning of it all. But one day he made a profound discovery that almost blew his mind. "Though I were perfect, yet would I not know my soul: I would despise my life" (Job 9:21).

What a hopeless thought! Here I am, spending all my time trying to understand myself and all my imperfections and weaknesses, and now I know that even if I were perfect—without a single fault—I still would not know my soul.

Even "perfect" people despise life at some time; people who are attractive; people who seem to have everything; people who seem to have no questions; people who appear well adjusted and successful. Even people who outwardly act like they know who they are; who can explain what life is all about; people with a purpose, who get things done; people who write the books and lecture about "How to cope"; yes—even people with "perfect" knowledge—really do not know their souls. They still face the same battles with despair, depression, loneliness, and temptations we all face. There are times they all face a crisis that causes them to despise what life puts them through.

This is the discovery this generation so fears today. What if, after all that seeking, all the searching, all the reading, all the struggle to learn—it won't really matter? The problems will still be there. The knowledge of who I am and why I am here may not change a thing. Could it be that all my life will be spent looking for a key that won't open anything? That horrible truth caused Job to "weary of life" (*see* Job 10:1).

A mind can spin off into madness trying to figure the meaning of life. And this generation will self-destruct if it keeps on wasting its time and energy seeking complete and perfect answers to life and its purpose. Job admitted his search only left him "full of confusion" (*see* Job 10:15). That confusion led him to the brink of suicide. ". . . Oh that I had given up the ghost, and no eye had seen me!" (Job 10:18).

High-school and college students by the thousands are committing suicide because their search for the meaning of life has left them confused and bitter. And the only antidote is to accept life as a gift from God.

Who am I? Why am I here? What's life all about? Who cares! Only when we see God face-to-face will we get the answers to these questions. But for now, spend your time learning how not to despise yourself and the life God has blessed you with. Be happy God has kept those secrets to Himself. Then let Him open your eyes to the revelation that perfect life is in Christ, and in Him we are complete. He is the answer to everything!

5. *A poor self-image and a fear of failure!* Job saw himself as a complete failure, careening into the ditch. "Even when I try hard, things still don't work out right for me," he said. "When I get a clean start and wash away all the past thoughts of failure, I always manage to mess things up."

> If I wash myself with snow water, and make my hands never so clean; Yet shalt thou plunge me in the ditch . . . .
>
> Job 9:30, 31

His self-image was devastated. He envied those around him "whose houses were safe from fear . . . who never have the rod of God upon them . . . whose children dance for joy . . . who spend their days in wealth and prosperity . . ." (*see* Job 21:9–13).

71

He pictured the world around him as being filled with happy, prosperous people, who lived ideal lives without fear or failure. Then he looked at his own life in comparison and saw nothing but a "mud-smeared" creature who was no better than dust. "He hath cast me into the mire, and I am become like dust and ashes" (Job 30:19).

Like most humans, Job had a terrible fear of failing. Even when he was successful and deeply engrossed in his work, the fear of failing was always there. When the crash came and he lost everything, he admitted to that lingering fear. He said: "For the thing which I greatly feared is come upon me, and that which I was afraid of is come unto me" (Job 3:25).

"It finally happened," thought Job. "Just as I always expected. I knew it was too good to be true. Someday the real me would mess everything up. I've had this nagging fear in me all along. I just didn't have it in me. I'm a failure." I meet these "failure freaks" all over the nation in my travels. They are "freaks" by their own admission. Too fat, too ugly, too skinny, too poor, too dumb.

A young lady in Chattanooga, Tennessee, came to me for help, advertising herself as "the worst failure you have ever met." She was a prostitute, an alcoholic, and a drug addict. Both hands were bandaged as a result of an unsuccessful suicide attempt. I listened for an hour to a truly sad life story.

Her mother killed herself when the girl was only five years old. She survived on the streets. Her eyes were blackened, the result of a fist blow from a barroom acquaintance. She dropped out of school and lived, without a friend, for years. She was, without a doubt, the most bombed-out creature I had ever seen. She looked me right in the eye and said, "Look at me, if you can. I'm an animal. I've tried killing myself at least four times, and tomorrow I'm going to try again. This time, nobody can stop me."

"Why," I asked, "do you and your generation so frequently want to commit suicide?"

Her answer echoed the despair of Job. "I just don't

like me—at all! I hate myself. I'm no good! And most of those I drink and shoot drugs with feel the same way. They do drugs and get drunk just so they can live with themselves. They aren't down on society, or the church, or their parents—just on themselves."

Job said it. The addicted say it. And all who contemplate suicide say it—"I don't like me!" What a wasted trip. Because all those other people Job envied— the successful, happy, involved people around him— were mostly all going through the same battle with fear as he was.

A twenty-one-year-old college beauty queen with a top grade average committed suicide. The note she left read, "I can't go on living with myself. I'm so unattractive. Nobody loves me. I'll never be what I want to be."

Those who knew her were visibly shaken. One coed said, "Wow, and all this time I've been jealous of her. She seemed to have everything going for her. She was really beautiful, smart, and well dressed. I didn't think she had a problem in the world. Who would have known she was so down on herself?"

There is only one way to overcome the debilitating effects of failure fears. Everybody on this planet has a few "structural weaknesses." We must learn to accept gracefully what we are and how we are made. Remember, too, everybody else is in the same boat. The Word of God says, "There hath no temptation taken you but such as is common to man . . ." (1 Corinthians 10:13). It is not some strange thing that has happened to you.

6. *Deep hurt caused by the loss of love from friends and family*. Not only did Job feel abandoned by a distant God, he also felt the deep hurt of close friends who turned on him. Even his own family misunderstood him. "My friends scorn me . . . All my inward friends abhorred me: and they whom I loved are turned against me" (Job 16:20; 19:19).

This is the sadness of suicide. A boyfriend just walks away and picks up with someone else. A sweetheart

73

sends her lover a note saying, "I don't want to see you again. It's all over." A close friend causes hurt by lying and cheating. Parents don't even try to understand. Even brothers and sisters act like enemies.

Job felt like a stranger in his house. He said, "My brethren are far from me, and my acquaintance are verily estranged from me. My kinsfolk have failed, and my familiar friends have forgotten me. They that dwell in my house . . . count me for a stranger: I am an alien in their sight . . . My wife, my children, despise me . . . they spake against me" (*see* Job 19:13–18).

No wonder Job cried out in agony, "Oh that I might have my request; and that God would grant me the thing that I long for! Even that it would please God to destroy me; that he would let loose his hand, and cut me off!" (Job 6:8, 9). Where there is no love, there seems to be no purpose to living. When he saw his friends and loved ones forsaking him, Job wanted to die and "go down into the pit."

Why do friends and loved ones often let you down when trouble and hard times fall on you? Why do they forsake you when the going gets rough? Why do those you trust the most often treat you like a stranger when you are down and out? Why are so many good friends only there in fair weather? Why do they forsake you just when you need them the most? Why do neighbors and acquaintances mock you when it looks like you are failing? Why do even close family members make you feel inferior when you are not on top?

Job figured it all out! He discovered a fact of life that explains why people don't want to be around someone who is "slipping." Job said, "He that is ready to slip with his feet is as a lamp despised in the thought of him that is at ease" (Job 12:5). Bluntly put, it means people who are comfortable and successful hate being around someone who is on his way down. The success cultists despise being around any negative forces. They don't want to associate with what they call "losers." It might rub off.

In essence, they are saying, "You may be on your way down—you may be thinking of quitting—but don't drag me down with you."

Job's friends saw his terrible condition; they looked on his despair and confusion and decided to keep their distance, lest they end up like him. They went on their way, putting poor, misguided Job out of their thoughts. As if just thinking about his downfall would infect them!

Does it surprise you that Job knew so much about being let down by those called friends and lovers? Have you experienced that deep hurt of getting kicked in the face by those you thought loved you? If so, what do you do? End it all? Many do!

Janet did. She was fifteen years old, and her boyfriend dropped her for someone else. She wrote, "Sir, I really loved Jimmy. I hoped to have married him someday. My whole world was wrapped up in him. I told my parents I had nothing left to live for and was going to kill myself. They laughed. They said it was just puppy love and someone else would come along to take his place. My minister told me it takes time to heal a broken heart. But I don't have time. Unless you can help me, I'll kill myself."

I tried calling Janet, unsuccessfully. Meanwhile, I sent her a special delivery, airmail letter stating, "Do nothing until you call me collect. Open this letter and call the enclosed number immediately. I'm waiting for your call—I can help."

The letter was returned to me, unopened. It must have been her parents who scribbled the note across the back of the returned envelope: "Send no more mail. Janet is no longer with us. She took her life."

If all others forsake and fail you, ". . . there is a friend that sticketh closer than a brother" (Proverbs 18:24). Jesus Christ is that Friend. And we are so much His friend, He laid down His life for us. If you had no other friend but Him, you would never be lonely again. Jesus said:

. . . I have called you friend . . . . I have chosen
you . . . If the world hate you, it hated me before it
hated you . . . I will send you comfort . . . .

See John 15:15–18, 26

A Light at the End of the Tunnel

What do you say to a person about to commit suicide?
How can they be stopped? Even more to the point, how
can we stop people from even flirting with suicidal
thoughts?

Too often we are so caught up in our counseling
techniques, we miss the truth. Truth alone sets troubled
minds free—not advice, not personal illustrations, not
heavy preaching or dogmatic fundamentals. We are so
into Freud, we can't get into the simple truth of Christ.
We have more confidence in our word of wisdom than in
the power of the Gospel. There is nothing worse than an
"expert" who is positive that he alone has all the answers
and that his word is "divinely inspired—straight from
God!"

Job was visited in his time of trouble by a group of
would-be counselors. They came to analyze him and
conduct "sessions" to help him get his head together.
They were determined to trace all the steps that led to his
difficulties. They were going to go back, way back, into
all the dark corners of his mind and retrace all the ugly
steps that brought about his trauma. Job dreaded such
tactics, and he said to them, "Withdraw thine hand far
from me: and let not thy dread make me afraid" (Job
13:21).

Don't Look Back

Those sincere and well-meaning "hurt healers" hoped
to isolate the root sin by probing and digging into Job's
past. They wanted him to replay all the demoralizing
steps that brought him to the ash heap.

"Job," they said, "there has to be a reason for your

mental attitude toward God and life. You must have a deep, hidden grudge against God or a friend. You must have sinned terribly, way back. God would not put you through all this sorrow and pain unless you have locked up some horrible secrets in your mind. Let's unlock those secrets and discover the cause of your pain." Read their interrogation of Job, and you will find it all there.

But Job would have none of it. "Is it good that he should search you out?" (Job 13:9). He rebuked them saying, ". . . ye are all physicians of no value" (Job 13:4). In other words, "You cannot help me by making me flash back into my past. You search for pride, for past failure, for old grievances—but I don't want to dig up dead memories."

God also disapproved of the probing methods of Job's sitters. God warned them, ". . . ye have not spoken of me the thing that is right . . ." (Job 42:7). God promised to deal with their advice of "folly" unless they repented and offered a sacrifice for their misguided judgment (*see* Job 42:8).

Jesus understood what Job meant. He once looked upon a poor, condemned adulteress and said nothing. No lectures. No probing into her past to find the root cause of her sinful ways. No tracing of steps that led to prostitution. Jesus gave no thought to the past. He forgave the past, wiped the slate clean, and said, "Go and sin no more."

In other words, "Start new, right now. Don't dig up the past; it's all forgiven. This is the first day of a new beginning. Go in peace and change your ways."

All hope begins with forgetting the past. Forget all your yesterdays. Never flash back. Don't dig up dead bones. Don't go scuba diving in the "sea of forgetfulness" and try to bring to the surface all those sins already forgiven and forgotten. Don't grieve the Saviour by trying to uncover sins already covered by His shed blood.

Paul said, ". . . this one thing I do, forgetting those things which are behind, and reaching forth unto those

77

things which are before, I press toward . . ." (Philippians 3:13, 14).

Jesus taught His disciples never to look back. Jesus said, "No man, having put his hand to the plow, and looking back, is fit for the kingdom of God" (Luke 9:62). So, if God remembers our past no more—why should we dwell on it?

Serve God and Get Rich Again

These heathen, successful counselors of Job propounded a shady theology. They believed in a God of kings, of winners, of strength and might, of success and riches. One of them, Elihu, enthusiastically stated that people who walk in God's ways obediently ". . . spend their days in prosperity, and their years in pleasures" (Job 36:11).

In other words, they were saying to Job, "If you understood the true nature of God, if you were living in a way pleasing to Him, you would be successful, and your life would be one beautiful pleasure after another. God is success and pleasure."

It was an insult to Job. Elihu was calling him a hypocrite, who was going to die a failure, simply because he was not thinking positive thoughts about how to be successful and enjoy life. Eliphaz, the Temanite, took this "God-is-profit" theology a step further. To him, the bottom line was gold and plenty of silver, to all who live good and think right. He said to Job, "If thou return to the Almighty, thou shalt be built up . . . Then shalt thou lay up gold as dust . . . Yea, the Almighty shall be thy defence, and thou shalt have plenty of silver" (Job 22:23–25).

No wonder God called their advice "dark counsel . . . words without knowledge" (see Job 38:2). How sad to hear this same shallow theology being pushed from pulpits today. It's an insult to a lowly Jesus, who became poor, who died a failure in the eyes of the world. It is this kind of materialistic preaching that has so ill-prepared an entire generation to endure any kind of pain—to be content with such things as they have—to be abased and not always abounding. Serving God becomes a kind of Olympic race, in which everyone must strive for the gold medals.

No wonder our young people give up in defeat. They can't live up to the image created by religion, of a happy-go-lucky, rich, successful, always positive-thinking Christian. Their world is not that idealistic. They look in a mirror reflecting a face covered with ugly pimples. They live with heartbreaks, hour-by-hour crises, and horrible family problems. Their friends are hooked and dying on all sides. They look into the uncertain future, frightened and worried. Loneliness, fear, and depression hound them daily.

Positive thinking won't make their problems go away. Saying these problems don't really exist doesn't change a thing. These "apostles of the positive" dare not exclude the Gethsemane experiences of life. The cup of pain, the hour of isolation, and the night of confusion were all part of the Master's life-style. Our great achievements, our successes, ought to take place at Gethsemane, not Fort Knox!

The sawdust trail has, for many, become the gold-dust trail. The Bible has become a catalog, with unlimited order blanks for life's goodies—for everyone who wants to become a "silver" saint. Anything having to do with Job-like pain and suffering is considered negative living. What pious claims are used to back up this theology. Elihu claimed to be speaking on God's behalf. He said to Job: ". . . he that is perfect in knowledge is with thee" (Job 36:4).

Apparently, God was speaking of Himself. God is good, and those who give generously do receive abundant blessings. One should always think on good and honest reports; but pain, poverty, and suffering have befallen sons of the saintliest of God's people—just like righteous Job.

When healing finally came to Job, he discovered gold, glory, or success was not what he wanted at all. All Job wanted was a faith in God which no disappointment in life could shake. He wanted to mean it when he said: "Though he slay me, yet will I trust in him . . ." (Job 13:15).

Job's Cry for Help

Job was ready to reach out and press on to find hope. He suggested three things that would help bring him back from the brink of death. In what Job said, we can know how to reach potential suicidals.

1. *Don't be afraid of my condition!* Job didn't want help from anyone who was overwhelmed by his pitiful condition. He stopped his experts counsel in the middle of their prattling and said, "For now ye are nothing; ye see my casting down, and are afraid" (Job 6:21).

Job must have been a pitiful sight. Here was a highly respectable man, who once sat as a judge at the gate of the city. People revered his wisdom and held him in high esteem. He had been the wealthiest, most successful man of his generation. But a series of tragedies brought him to poverty. His influence was gone. Young men ridiculed him. No one sought his advice. Instead, he sat alone, covered with open boils. He lived in constant pain, covered with pockmarks—the father of ten children who had died by sword, fire, and hurricane. The troubles of Job became the talk of the nation.

Job discerned hypocrisy in those who came to "comfort and help" him. He said to them, "You see my hopeless condition and it overwhelms you. You really don't believe I'll ever come out of it. You think I'm too far gone. You can't help me, because you come to me with fear. You know only a miracle can save me, but you don't believe that a man so low as I will ever experience that miracle. Deep in your heart you are saying, 'Job will

80

always be a broken, poor man.' "

I've experienced what Job was talking about. A broken-down addict or alcoholic sits in my presence, talking about suicide. He is dirty, sick, and already half dead. His mind is in a fog. Yet, he begs for help. I look at him, thinking to myself, "Dear God, I've seen you change people like this—but this one? Look at him! He's just a shell. How can You do anything with such a wreck? Can he really be healed and become a clean, holy vessel of honor?"

Unless we who offer help can believe in miracles—unless we can look these distraught people right in the eye with hope and faith—unless we can get our eyes off their terrible present condition and see what they can be—then we are also "physicians of no value."

What the suicidal person is saying is, "Don't look at me like that! Talk to me like you know I can be helped. And I'll know if you're just talking theory or if you really speak in faith."

2. *Don't try to overwhelm me with reproof!* Job was tired of all the talking. He didn't want to talk about his problems anymore, and he wanted no one preaching at him. He said, ". . . I will lay mine hand upon my mouth. Once I have spoken; but I will not answer . . . I will proceed no further" (Job 40:4, 5).

Right words at the right time are very forcible, according to Job. But arguing proves nothing. Words of reproof to a desperate man are like the wind (*see* Job 6:26). How right he is! We jump all over troubled people with reproof. "Get hold of yourself! Quit acting like a child! Grow up! Don't make God mad with all your foolish talk about giving up. Shape up and start acting normal."

Job had been talking like a defeated man. His conversation was preoccupied with sorrow, trouble, fear, and hopelessness. But all the experts could say to him was: "Quit talking like that! You can't really mean it. You are just trying to shock people!"

But Job knew he was not lying or putting up a false

front. He was speaking from his heart. And he wanted everybody to quit reproving him for giving vent to his hurt.

How very difficult it has been for me to heed the warning of Job. I listen for a while, then I jump in and try to overpower the poor, troubled person with an avalanche of Scriptures, personal experiences, and words of advice. But what that person really wants and needs is a good listening ear. It's a way to relieve grief. It can't stay bottled up. Job said, ". . . if I hold my tongue, I shall give up the ghost" (Job 13:19). Meaning, "If I keep it all inside me, I'll die."

Job went a step further. He wanted his counselors to trade places with him. With disdain, he said to them, "Ye are all miserable comforters . . . all you do is speak endlessly vain words" (*see* Job 16:2, 3). "Put yourself in my place," he said. "Try to understand me from where I am—not from where you sit."

> . . . if your soul were in my soul's stead, I could heap up words against you, and shake mine head at you. But I would strengthen you with my mouth, and the moving of my lips should assuage your grief.
>
> Job 16:4, 5

How clearly put! " If you were in my place, I could pile up a heap of sermons on you, too! I could take on that holier-than-thou attitude also. But I wouldn't! Instead, I'd use every word carefully to comfort you and help chase the grief away."

3. *Pity me!*

> To him that is afflicted pity should be shewed from his friend . . . .
>
> Job 6:14

Pity is compassion for someone else's suffering. It can become a form of love, if it helps alleviate sorrow and suffering. The kind of pity Job sought was far more than a condescending sympathy. To pity someone in a spiritual way is to be aroused by their condition to the point of more than a casual involvement. True pity says, "I'm in this with you all the way."

Job cried out from the depths of his agony, "Have pity upon me, have pity upon me, O ye my friends; for the hand of God hath touched me" (Job 19:21). He was calling for others to make a vicarious identification with him. It is the same kind of pity the heavenly Father shows toward His children. He hurts with us. He is touched with the feelings of our infirmities.

Breaking it down, it simply means a troubled, hurt person needs at least one friend who will stick with him through all the highs and lows. It's a cry from the afflicted soul, saying to friends and family, "Don't give up on me. Show me just a little pity until I get through my battle. Don't reject me just because I'm depressed and confused. Be patient. I need you."

Oh, God! Give me that kind of pity. Let me weep with the brokenhearted. Let me listen with love. Let me be there to lean on when they are low.

9

Solving Your Problem

Job's real victory was conquering himself. Ultimately, his help did not come from others. He helped himself. The solution to his problems came from his desperation. It was not what some intelligent friend or expert said to him that brought healing—it was an awakening in his spirit. It was a rebirth of his doing.

A whirlwind message came directly to Job from God. "Gird up your loins now like a man" (*see* Job 40:6, 7). God intervened. He was saying to Job, "It's time to get hold of yourself. You've been down in the pit long enough. It's time to walk out of this cave. Prepare to act like a new person."

Job began to realize he would never find the right kind of help from those around him—not from his family, nor his close associates, nor from the many physicians who kept prescribing useless therapy. "If I am ever going to come out of this tailspin, I'll have to take the first step myself," he concluded. "I've had enough; I can't take another minute of this life of confusion and disorder. I'm going to stand up now against the whole world and pick myself up from the dust."

Job's desire to help himself is completely scriptural. ". . . work out your own salvation with fear and trembling. For it is God which worketh in you both to will and to do of his good pleasure" (Philippians 2:12, 13). "For every man shall bear his own burden" (Galatians 6:5).

Job began to realize there was as much of God in him as in those around him. "ut I have understanding as well as you; I am not inferior to you . . ." (Job 12:3). He would go it alone, with God on his side. "Is not my help in me? . . ." (Job 6:13).

And when God saw Job was ready to trust Him again, things began to happen in quick order. Job experienced a great miracle in his life. Not only were his mind and body healed, his attitudes changed, and all thoughts of death expelled—he was soon back on top. The Bible makes that clear: "So the Lord blessed the latter end of Job more than his beginning . . . And the Lord turned the captivity of Job . . ." (Job 42:12, 10). He ended up with twice as much as he had before; happier, more fulfilled.

But how did this miracle of deliverance come about? What turns a despondent, broken person into a right-thinking one with purpose? What does a person have to do in order to experience that same kind of changed life? What are the secrets?

I am realizing, more than ever, that people with suicidal thoughts want more than talk. They want simple and direct answers to help them come out of the fog. A seventeen-year-old girl wrote: "Sir, your messages on suicide are very helpful, but we need more than words—we need answers. Tell us how to overcome these urges." And that is exactly why I am using God's Holy Word to show us what those honest answers are.

Job did four simple things, all on his own, to initiate change in his life. And any troubled person today can see the same results in his life if he follows these same four steps:

1. *He began to believe that God really is, and that He does answer prayer!*

. . . he that cometh to God must believe that he is, and that he is a rewarder of them that diligently seek him.

Hebrews 11:6

Job made a confession that saved his life and changed it completely. He looked to God and proclaimed, "I know that thou canst do every thing . . ." (Job 42:2). He caught a glimpse of the bigness and greatness of God.

God had taken Job into the Spirit world and revealed to him the unfathomable power behind nature. He was shown the foundations of the earth; the law of the sea that kept it from covering the earth; the miracle of new mornings; the place where light sprang forth to light the earth; the treasure house of snow, hail, and wind; the celestial watercourse that caused it to rain on the wilderness when it's thirsty; the gendering of ice and frost; the innumerable stars and galaxies stretching over the dominion of space; the ordinances of lightning, thunder, clouds, and rainbows; the laws of instinct and rhythm that govern nature and the creatures of the earth; the mysterious ways of the whole animal kingdom; the intrigues of the deep sea; and the perfect harmony of nature, the earth, and the universe.

Job was left breathless after this vision of God's awesome power over all the forces that govern the earth and all mankind. It began to dawn on Job, "If God is that great—if He controls oceans and all the creatures therein—if He knows every animal by name—if He creates mountains and galaxies—if He feeds the birds and all earth's creatures—does He not have more than enough power to help me? If God can create and control the heavens, He can control the flow of our life—God is there! He is great! He has unlimited power! What is my little problem in comparison to His great power? He can do everything, anything."

Job moved out of his troubled little world, into God's vast kingdom. "God," he said, "You were there all the time; I just couldn't see You, or feel You, or find You. You were there, taking care of the universe; feeding the birds, the fish in the sea, and guiding the galaxies and the universe in its course. Now I know You are bigger than all my problems."

He realized also there is no such thing as an unanswered prayer. There are only "uncompleted" ones. God is in the process of completing every prayer lifted to Him in faith.

Job moved out of his suicidal despair before he saw even a single prayer answered. No miracle had happened. No mountains had moved. No boils had healed. No children were raised from the dead. His friends were still cold toward him. There was not one sign—not one fleece fulfilled—no earthshaking change—no overnight cure—just simple faith in God's great power! And even though Job had not received any answers to his prayers as yet, he declared, "I have heard of thee by the hearing of the ear: but now mine eye seeth thee" (Job 42:5). Job was now ready to believe that God not only hears and answers prayer, but that He was also a mind reader, who knew what Job needed even before he asked. ". . . no thought can be withholden from thee" (Job 42:2).

Job was no longer talking doubt and defeat. Nothing changed but his attitude toward God. This broken-down man, who had been moaning, "I suffer a destruction from God . . . on my eyelids is the shadow of death (*see* Job 16:11–16), now shouts in triumph, "Now mine eye seeth *Him!*" When you get your eyes on Him, you no longer see only yourself.

2. *He harnessed his hate!*

Wherefore I abhor myself . . . .
Job 42:6

You ask, "How can Job be on the mend if he is still talking about despising himself? Isn't that a clue that he is still dwelling on his failure? If he had moved out of his world of despair unto the realm of faith, why is he still hating himself? What kind of healing is that?"

Job had been so full of hate. Remember what he said? "I curse my day . . . Let the day perish wherein I was born . . . I am wicked, no good . . . So I deserve this strange punishment . . ." (*see* Job 3:3). Isn't he the man who so despised and loathed his life he said, ". . . my soul chooseth strangling, and death rather than my life" (Job 7:15)?

Here now is that same man, confessing once again, "I hate myself. I despise me!" Shouldn't he be shaking off all that self-hate? If he is to be truly healed of all his hurts, shouldn't he be saying to himself and the world, "I am finished with putting myself down!"? If he is coming out of the pit, where is his improved self-image?

Here is where we must stop for a moment and take a closer look at some hard facts.

The truth is, you cannot just "shake off" doubts, fears, despair, and self-hatred. Make all the promises you please, turn over as many "new leaves" as you choose, promise yourself you will "grit your teeth" and think right—none of it really works. Self-determination will never shake off self-hatred. You can't be healed with good intentions alone. I have seen alcoholics weep, pray, and then promise "never to touch another drop of booze." But they go right out and get stoned. More than anything in the world, they wanted to quit drinking. There was an agonizing cry deep within them for healing. But they revert to the bottle because they try to eradicate "the demon of drink," rather than try to harness the hate in them that drove them to drink in the first place.

Now let us look at what Job said in a new light. Yes—he did say, "I abhor myself." But this was now a "harnessed hate." He was now in control, redirecting his hate. It was no longer a hatred of himself for being a failure. He was not despising himself for past sins. No! Job was actually saying, "I hate the way I've been hating. I'm ashamed of being ashamed. I've been wrong. I've been hating myself all along for the wrong reasons. I hate myself now for not realizing I was in God's care all the time. I despise the fact that I allowed myself to buy the devil's lies. I am grieved because I allowed myself to be such a doubter for so long. I hate the way I flirted with death. I hate that I wasted so much time feeling sorry for myself." In modern slang, Job was saying, "I could kick myself for being so stupid!" To harness means to "bring under control and direct the force of."

That is all you can do with your hate and your wild thoughts. The Word of God warns us all to be "bringing into captivity every thought to the obedience of Christ" (2 Corinthians 10:5). Direct its force! Or, make your hate behave.

Hatred is like a mighty energy force out of control. It can be useful if controlled and trained. The best riding horses are wild stallions that have been broken, trained, and harnessed.

Job didn't pray, "Oh, God, take this hate out of my heart. Strip me of my bad temper, and take all the thoughts of death out of my mind!" He took an honest look into his heart and saw hatred and evil thoughts about God's faithfulness. Rather than fight that hate, he accepted it, then set about to remake it, so that it could do him some good. He was saying, in reality, "I know I am capable of hating. I know how to hate with fury. I am good at building walls around me that no one can penetrate. I am good at not letting people reach me. So—I am going to turn it all around and use that hatred to build new walls. Walls against despair. Walls against letting people affect me wrongly. Walls to protect me from thoughts of failure. I am going to hate even the slightest thought of being forsaken by God. I am going to abhor and despise the devil and all his lies! I am going to be good at hating with fury all thoughts of suicide. I am going to make my hate work for me. I will now be the master of my feelings."

Hate and despair no longer controlled Job's life. Instead, Job took command and made every thought and feeling fall in line obediently.

3. *He quit justifying himself!*

Then Job answered the Lord, and said, Behold, I am vile; what shall I answer thee? I will lay mine hand upon my mouth. Once have I spoken; but I will not answer: yea, twice; but I will proceed no further.

Job 40:3–5

"I have come to the end of myself," Job was confessing. "I will proceed no further." Up to this very time, Job believed he had every right to complain. He had a right to express his despair. He had a right to be angry and bitter. He had a right to take his life into his hands. After all, life dealt him nothing but trouble. Fate had stacked the cards against him. He didn't have a chance. He was reacting like any normal person would when swamped with nothing but trouble.

To his friends, Job had been arguing, "But you just don't understand. You don't know what I'm going through. I didn't ask to be in this position—it was forced on me." But that was all over now. Job said, "I'm going to cover my mouth and quit making excuses. I'm going to be honest with God and myself."

Job repented! He was sorry for trying to hide from the truth. He forced himself to forget the past, to quit making excuses for being down, and to immediately stop pitying himself.

That is the very point at which healing begins for every despairing person. It begins when you are ready to stop making excuses for the way you have been acting. Quit trying to prove you are right. Stop all the talking, and quit making alibis. Start admitting your attitudes are all wrong.

Job was saying to God, "I am vile, I have sinned, but I'm sorry. I repent, and I want to change." He swallowed his pride.

I have discovered lately that almost everyone who comes to me for help to overcome suicidal urges is proud. They are despondent, in trouble, but very proud. Underneath all the talk of failure, under the veneer of a poor self-image, is a fountain of pride. It is the pride that always goes before destruction.

A businessman called me recently and poured out a woeful story of trouble. Everything was going wrong. Everybody was lying about him. People were jealous. Nothing seemed to work out right. Debts were piling up.

Creditors were hounding him. Everywhere he turned, he got a cold shoulder—so he said. But when I asked if I could share in his suffering and lend him enough money to keep food on his table, he responded angrily, "Forget it. I can make my own way. I'm a good provider, and I don't want any of your welfare. Things are just great. Everything's fine. Good-bye."

The man was broke. He was at the end of himself. He needed that loan. He needed to admit his need. But no! He was too proud to admit he needed help.

That is exactly why so many people today can never be helped. They will go from bad to worse. They will grow in bitterness and fear, because they are too proud to admit they need help. They want to make it all on their own. They can't cry in front of people. They don't want others to think they are weak.

But Job became teachable. Before now, he was trying to work out everything all by himself. It's true, we help ourselves. It's true, the answers are within us. But what we learn on our own is to become teachable—to listen. We learn to swallow our pride.

Some people make idols of their perplexities and problems. They even boast about their confusion. One such lady bragged to me, "Why, Sir, I've been to dozens of psychiatrists. I've talked to ministers everywhere I go. All my friends have tried to help me. But I'm incurable. You won't be able to help me, because no one else has yet succeeded. I'm hopeless." That spirit must be broken. Teachableness is the first sign of honesty.

Some think their problems are so much more serious and complicated—therefore, the solutions that work for others just don't apply to them. Theirs is a more "intellectual," sophisticated problem—far different from the problems of the masses.

Some, who claim to be humbly seeking help, are simply dishonest. They are not really prepared to hear and obey the truth. They prefer to play the game of "seeking, but never finding." The pursuit of truth is more important to them than finding it. Once they face the truth, they have no other mask to hide behind. It is their way of never facing reality. It's a "selfish delight."

Quit asking for help until you are prepared to act! What hypocrisy—you go everywhere seeking guidance, asking for counsel, sharing your deep personal problem—but you never hear a word. You talk but never listen. You are not prepared to accept the truth—and not even an angel from heaven, with a direct message from God, can reach you!

You claim to have suffered more pain than others. You claim no one understands your agony and despair—yet you choose to forget all the martyrs who were murdered in their quest for peace and joy. You are not the only one suffering—others all around you carry deep hurts. There is nothing that has happened to you that isn't common to all men. You are not going through some "strange and mysterious" trial—unique and precisely yours.

We must become, like Paul the apostle, a helpless cripple and allow others to "take us by the hand and lead us" (*see* Acts 13:11). There is hope for the humble.

4. *He became concerned for others!*

> And the Lord turned the captivity of Job, when he prayed for his friends . . . .
>
> Job 42:10

This is the final step to healing. Do more than forgive your friends and family. Get concerned about their needs. Pray for them. Make a mental list of everyone who mistreated you: those who walked away when you needed them the most, those who cheated on you, misused you, and treated you like dirt. Then go down that list, one by one, forgiving them from your heart. Then pray for them. Pray God will bless and prosper them. Pray that God will allow you to help them in some way. That, positively, will bring glorious health and strength to you. That is the way to complete healing.

93

Be mad at no one! Get rid of every grudge. For when you forgive others, Jesus forgives you. When you pray for others, God begins to answer you. God turns captivity into freedom. Praying for others unlocks the chains on your own mind. It floods your soul with unbelievable joy and peace. You become a new person. People will not believe you are the same person. They will say to you, "What happened? You're different. You are not the same person."

Job could have asked God for revenge, but instead, he opened his arms and said, "Welcome back." And when you welcome those who hurt you, the whole world welcomes the new you.

Job did not need their advice or preaching—but he did need their love. Everybody needs love; we all need friends. But the Bible says, "He that would have friends must show himself to be friendly" (*see* Proverbs 18:24). When you start thinking of others, they start thinking of you. When you begin to care for others, they begin to care for you.

There is nothing complicated about Job's reach to recovery. The truth has been made so simple, even a child can understand it. Job took the necessary steps to freedom, and things finally began to happen. ". . . the Lord gave Job twice as much as he had before. So the Lord blessed the latter end of Job more than his beginning . . ." (Job 42:10, 12).

Twice as much—better than before! That is the way God works. And what God did for Job, He wants to do for every troubled soul. He wants to make you better than you were before the trouble started. He wants not only to turn things around and heal your mind, He wants to make things even better than you ever had it! Believe it—it's all yours!

10

A Suicide Checklist

Suicide is such a thoughtless act. I am convinced a majority of suicides could be prevented if people contemplating it would only give it more thought. So many have killed themselves in haste, never once thinking of the consequences.

For those thinking of suicide, I have devised a simple checklist of things to do first. Every thought of suicide should be set aside until all of these things have been done. Take the following steps, and your attitude about suicide should come into clear focus.

1. *Pretend blindness for three hours.* Cover both eyes with bandages and tape them shut. Pretend you are blind for just three hours. Walk around and try to do the things you normally would. Live in that darkness, bumping and feeling your way around the house.

Imagine what it must be like to be blind. Try to experience the thoughts of a blind person. Think of never again seeing color, or sunlight, or trees and flowers. Think of what it would be like to spend the rest of your life unable to see anything. Think blind for those three hours.

Sometimes you can see things clearer in a short period of blindness. It happened that way to Saul, immediately after his conversion. He was three days without sight when Ananias came to pray for his healing. In that time of blindness, he saw himself as he really was. He realized he was fighting for a wrong cause. He realized he was angry for the wrong reasons. He admitted to strong but misdirected feelings. He began to see things he'd never seen before. He saw Jesus as a Friend and not an enemy. He also saw "how great things he must suffer" (*see* Acts 9:1–16).

I would hope, in your temporary blindness, you could see Jesus as your Friend, too. You should begin to realize how fortunate you are to be able to see. You may be depressed, but you can still see. If you can thank God for nothing else, you can thank Him for your sight.

When you take off the blindfold, think of how Satan tries to plunge people into darkness. Then remember the words of Jesus,

> Yet a little while is the light with you. Walk while ye have the light, lest darkness come upon you: for he that walketh in darkness knoweth not whither he goeth. While ye have light, believe in the light, that ye may be the children of light . . . .
>
> John 12:35, 36

2. *Buy a bunch of grapes.* I mean just that. Purchase a full cluster of grapes and take them to the privacy of your room. Hold those grapes in your hand and just look at them for a few minutes. Then think of the vine in some vineyard that bore them. Think of the branch from which they were plucked. Think of the sun and rain putting nutrients into the soil, the vine drawing out those nutrients, which then flow into each branch and finally into the cluster—even into each little grape.

Foolish? Not at all. Jesus said He is "the true vine," and we are the branches. The life that is in Christ flows into us. The grapes are the fruit we bear.

Now squeeze a few of those grapes, letting the juices and the pulp fall into a cup. Consider what you have done. You have squeezed out the life of those grapes. That is how I picture suicide—an act of squeezing out the life before it could do any good.

Isaiah, the prophet, declared God looked upon life as a cluster of grapes intended to bless. "Thus saith the Lord, As the new wine is found in the cluster, and one saith, Destroy it not; for a blessing is in it: so will I do for my servants' sakes, that I may not destroy them all" (Isaiah 65:8).

God is talking about life—your life. "Don't destroy it; there's a blessing in it." You have the power in your hand to destroy that cluster of grapes, but God made grapes to be a blessing. You may be down and out. You may think you are worthless. You may see yourself as untalented and good-for-nothing. But God sees what you are inside. "There is a blessing in it." Your life will yet help others. You must not destroy yourself in any way—because God put that power to bless in you, and it will come forth in time. The tombstone of every completed suicide should read, "Buried with untapped blessings."

3. *Prepare your arguments for the Judgment Day*. Get a sheet of paper and write out a prepared statement, listing all the excuses you plan to give the Lord on the Judgment Day. Or have you not yet heard that after death we all go to the Judgment? The Bible says, "So then every one of us shall give account of himself to God . . . . for we shall all stand before the judgment seat of Christ" (Romans 14:12, 10).

What will you tell the Judge? You have to answer for what you do. You will be forced to explain. Every eye will see that Judge; every knee will bow to Him; and every tongue will answer for every deed done in the flesh.

Write it on paper and memorize it. Tell God all about why you gave up. Tell Him you had a Bible in your room, but that you didn't believe it was true. Tell Him how you didn't believe He was hearing you. Explain to Him about all the wasted tears you shed. Tell Him all about how you planned entering eternity at your own choosing. Say to Him, "Lord, I had to do it. You let me down. There were no guardian angels. There was no plan for me. Nobody understood me. Life was no longer worth living. Only the devil was real. I was empty, lonely, and depressed. And even though You said You'd never leave or forsake any of Your children—You lost me! So You see, Lord, I had to do it."

Why not write your reasons for committing suicide? Why not list all the arguments for doing it? God wants to

97

hear what you have to say. The Bible says, "Produce your cause, saith the Lord; bring forth your strong reasons, saith the King of Jacob" (Isaiah 41:21). After writing down all the reasons and after preparing a statement to present to the righteous Judge on that final day, then write these words across the bottom of the page: "For by thy words thou shalt be justified, and by thy words thou shalt be condemned" (Matthew 12:37).

4. *Fake a cure.* It is foolish for a person to kill himself without at least imagining how things could have been, had he kept on living.

Pretend your depression has lifted and that all your worries have been laid on the Lord. Pretend God heard the cry of your heart and that all things are now working together for your good. Pretend you are really loved and people really do care about you. Pretend the person who hurt you so badly is really not that important to you, after all. Pretend all the hurts are healing and a new love has entered your life. A new love that is so much better than the old.

Make believe all God's promises are working, and God is beginning to hear you even before you ask. Make believe no one is talking about you behind your back. Imagine you are someone special to yourself and to God. Pretend there is a special someone who loves you. Pretend you know you will find that love.

Pretend a miracle has happened, and a way out of your jungle is beginning to appear. Make believe life is still precious; sunshine is beautiful; and the future is looking brighter.

Keep thinking like that for as long as you can. Even if you have to fake it. "For as he thinketh in his heart, so is he . . ." (Proverbs 23:7). Perhaps it will begin to dawn on you that there is no need to fake it. You might just realize that, if you commit the keeping of your future into the Lord's hand, you will enter into a glorious rest. Then, by faith alone, your cure can be real.

11

The Law Against Loneliness

I have a theory that suicide is a result of misdirected hunger pangs. Mankind was created with an innate hunger for God, which must be satisfied. God so longed for the companionship of the man and the woman He created, He caused the inner man to experience loneliness as a kind of magnet to draw him back into His presence.

He knew the power of sin to drive man out of His holy presence. Sin separates man from God. But God put within that man and woman an instinct. It is a very powerful instinct, which yearns at all times to return to the heavenly Father. And loneliness is the force that is designed to make that instinct work.

People everywhere are afraid of loneliness. It is feared as an enemy of body and soul. It is a powerful force, which drives homosexuals and lesbians to despair. Those involved in that life claim they experience a kind of loneliness that only few can comprehend. Often, it drives them to suicide. Addicts, alcoholics, and prostitutes live with overwhelming loneliness every waking hour. But all the time, it is God at work, wooing them back to Himself.

Even the holiest of Christians experience periods of loneliness. There comes an inner itch that can't be scratched. It is an emptiness that cannot be described. Because you can be lonely even in a crowd. You can be lonely when in the arms of someone you love. Some of the loneliest people I have ever met were walking through Times Square in the middle of the theater rush.

The Real Cause of Loneliness

Loneliness has nothing at all to do with isolation from people. I know of prisoners of war who were locked in solitary confinement for months, yet were not overcome by loneliness. Some of them were Christians who experienced the reality of Christ in those isolated dungeons.

Loneliness is caused by separation from the presence of God. That empty, lonely, depressed feeling is God's way of calling you back to Himself. When you grow cold toward God, when your faith weakens, when you quit feeding your soul with His Holy Word, when you no longer pray, when you neglect the things of the Spirit, you will become lonely. It is inevitable. Loneliness is God on the line, calling you to come quickly into His presence.

I know what that means. I've been in the ministry for years, and I've known Jesus Christ as Lord since I was a child. But I have, at times, experienced a strange kind of loneliness that has swept over me for apparently no reason.

I loved my wife and children dearly. I was surrounded by friends and people who loved and respected me. I preached to thousands and received mail from thousands more. But I felt lonely. I knew my loneliness was not a result of sin. It was not because I was unhappy or unfulfilled. I was not mad at anybody. Yet, I was lonely, and it kept hanging on. It was then I discovered this secret—that all loneliness is a result of having strayed a bit from His presence. I realized how busy I had become. I was crowded with duties that robbed me of time with God.

Instead of being shut in with God, I was overly busy with the details of everyday life. My Bible reading suffered as a result. My prayer life dwindled to "thinking prayers" only. I prayed in my head. They were thought prayers shot like quick arrows to the throne room of God. I had become a one-way servant to God. I was lonely because I was hungry for God. My appetite for God was just fine—it was just that I didn't take the time to satisfy those misdirected hunger pangs. The Bible says: ". . . in thy presence is fulness of joy; at thy right hand there are pleasures for evermore" (Psalms 16:11).

His presence is the law against loneliness. This fullness of joy expels all loneliness. When you come back into His presence—wanting nothing more than to love and worship Him—a miracle happens. The joy of the Lord becomes your strength. In that secret closet, shut in with God, we experience a miraculous lifting of despair and depression.

Unless those misdirected hunger pangs are satisfied and dispelled, they can lead to death. Only people who are dead spiritually can commit suicide. That is why it is so important to understand what causes loneliness.

There are Christians who do pray. They do read their Bibles faithfully, go to church regularly, and they are very busy doing God's work. But in spite of all their furious activity in the cause of Christ, they are still extremely lonely at times. Why? Because they have not yet known what it means to come into the Lord's presence just to listen.

Jesus Gets Lonely, Too

Believe it or not, even Jesus gets lonely! Get ready now to blow the lid off your theology. Be prepared to see Jesus in an entirely new light. Did you know we have been coming at our problems from the wrong end? We have been so preoccupied with our loneliness, we have not even entertained the thought our Lord gets lonely, too. And if we can understand His loneliness, we will soon get to the root of our own.

Our Lord has an almost insurmountable problem of communicating with those of us who claim to love Him so. He is a "feeling" Saviour, and His feelings and needs have been totally neglected by many of His children.

We seek to satisfy the heart of Jesus through praise only. We sing and shout and lift a chorus of worship and adoration, and that is wonderful and scriptural. We come unto His gates with praise and enter His courts with thanksgiving. We praise Him with instruments. We praise

101

Him with song, with uplifted hands, with tears, and loud hosannas. But it is still only one-way communication. God commands everything that has breath to praise Him. But praise alone does not meet our Saviour's need.

He Never Gets to Talk

I wonder if the Lord ever wearies of His children coming into His presence and never once stopping to listen. Nothing is so empty and unfulfilling as one-way communication. Try listening to someone for a few hours, without getting in a word. It leaves you with a feeling of loneliness. The person who "got the load off his chest" goes away feeling better—he talked it out. But the poor listener, who could not offer a single word of advice or share his own heart, stands there unfulfilled.

How often have we left our Lord there, alone in the secret closet, lonely and unfulfilled? We rush into His presence with a "Praise You, Jesus; worship You, Jesus! Glory to Jesus! Here's my shopping list and my healing card. Amen." How many times has He been so ready and anxious to open His own heart to speak, when lo and behold, no one was there?

If we pray an hour, we talk an hour. If we pray for hours, we talk for hours. If we pray all night, we talk all night. Millions of voices, talking, talking, and praising. All my preaching life has been spent in trying to get people to pray. Now, I see that has not really been the problem. The real problem is leaving the Saviour in the secret closet, alone, unfulfilled, lonely—having said not a word to us. We left that closet of prayer, having unburdened our hearts. We talked it all out with Him, joy filled our heart. We told Him of our hopes, dreams, desires. We left that holy place of prayer with a satisfied mind.

Yet, our Lord was still there, waiting with keen anticipation, longing to share in that communion. Does our Lord not say, "Yes, yes, thank you for your praise. I accept it. I'm so glad you took the time to be shut in with

Me. I heard your request, and the Father will give you the desire of your heart. But please wait! Please be still awhile. Don't leave just now. I have some things I want to share with you. My heart is yearning to be unburdened to you. I've bottled your tears; I've soothed your troubled mind. Now, allow Me to talk! Allow Me to tell you what is in My heart!''

Our Lord Jesus wants to talk. He wants to tell us what is breaking His heart in our generation. He wants to speak to each child about the beautiful plan He has for all who trust Him—revealing glorious truths; guidance for ourselves and help in raising children; solutions to problems; new ministries and outreaches that will save the lost; specific words concerning jobs, careers, homes, life partners; and truths about heaven, hell, and the coming calamities. Most of all, He wants to talk to us about how much He loves and cares for His own.

We Forget He Has a Need, Too

Lest you think I am unscriptural, listen to His words. Here is a beautiful glimpse into the heart of Jesus.

> But which of you, having a servant plowing or feeding cattle, will say to him . . . when he is come from the field, Go and sit down to meat? And will not rather say unto him, Make ready wherewith I may sup, and gird thyself, and serve me, till I have eaten and drunken; and afterward thou shalt eat and drink?
>
> Luke 17:7, 8

We have no trouble at all identifying with that servant in his duty to his master. No trouble in putting on our apron and serving up the Lord a full table of praises—a good feast of worship. We love to feed our Lord! We love to see Him feasting on our service and love. We gird ourselves, make ready, and serve Him with gladness. It is our greatest joy, our supreme fulfillment—to minister unto the Lord.

But we have difficulty with the last part—the Lord's part. "And afterward, you shall eat!" That is too much for us to comprehend. We do not know how to sit down after we have served Him—to allow Him the same joy we experienced in serving Him! We rob our Lord of the joy of ministering to us.

We think our Lord gets enough pleasure from what we do for Him. But there is so much more. Our Lord responds to our faith. He rejoices when we repent. He talks to the Father about us. He delights in our childlike trust. It pleases Him to give us rest and peace and to fulfill all His promises on our behalf. But I am convinced that His greatest need is to have a one-to-one personal communication with those He left here on earth. Not a single angel in heaven can meet that need. No one who has already passed the veil can meet that need. Jesus wants to talk to those on the battlefield. He must have open lines—two-way lines—to every soldier on every front.

Resurrected, but Lonely

Where did I get such a notion that Christ is lonely and has a desperate need to speak? It's all there in the beautiful account of Christ appearing to the two disciples on the road to Emmaus. Jesus had just been resurrected. The same day, about noon, Cleopas and another disciple were walking from Jerusalem to Emmaus—a distance of about six and one-half miles.

Jesus drew near. They were grieved about their departed Lord. In their grief, they did not recognize Him. To really understand the deep need in our Lord's heart, watch Him carefully as He walked beside those talking, grieving disciples. They were communing and reasoning between themselves.

How lonely Jesus must have been. He wanted to talk; He had so much to say to them. And when He could hold

104

back no longer, Jesus stopped listening and began talking:

> And it came to pass, that, while they communed together and reasoned, Jesus himself drew near, and went with them. And beginning at Moses and all the prophets, he expounded unto them in all the scriptures the things concerning himself.
>
> Luke 24:15, 27

There could have been no finer experience for those disciples. They heard His voice and went away saying, "Did not our heart burn within us, while he talked with us?"

But because we have never understood the needs of Jesus, we think only of the joy those disciples shared. What about the joy of Jesus? They said their hearts burned when He talked. But I see a resurrected Lord, tears streaming down His glorified cheeks, walking down that dusty road with a heart filled with joy. He was fulfilled; His need was met. While the world waited, Jesus interrupted the whole plan of redemption a few hours—just to talk! I see Jesus overjoyed. He had ministered. In His glorified form, He had experienced His first two-way communion. He poured out His heart. His lonely heart was touched. His need, too, had been met.

We Must Allow Him to Speak to Us

We know so little today about His voice and His need to speak to us. We are too occupied with His power, to be aware of His voice. Like Elijah, the great prophet, we are more familiar with demonstrations of power than we are of His still, small voice.

Elijah exercised the power of prayer. He closed and opened the heavens. He called fire down and parted waters with his mantle. A man of action, who brought entire governments under his spell, he stood on Mount Carmel and mocked the prophets of Baal, killing them right under the king's nose.

This mighty man of prayer enters God's throne room seven times, earnestly praying for rain. Seven times Elijah talks to God about this one need. A little cloud appears, and the prophet who, three and one-half years before, closed the heavens and caused a terrible drought, now opens the heavens and "an abundance" of rain falls.

Elijah outran Ahab's chariot over the sixteen miles to the royal residence. Elijah was flushed with victory. A great spiritual awakening was about to take place. The fire of God had fallen. Miracles had been witnessed by multitudes. It had been an unbelievable display of God's mighty power. Elijah thought, "Now, even Jezebel will repent! Even she cannot dismiss these signs and wonders. This is God's hour for this nation."

What a shock he got! Jezebel was not at all impressed with miracles and power. She said to Elijah, "By tomorrow at this time, I will kill you, just like you killed my priests."

The next time you see this great man of power and action—this mighty prayer warrior—this miracle worker—this man who calls fire down out of heaven—he is hiding in a cave almost two hundred miles away on Mount Horeb.

What a sight! Forty days and forty nights he spends, brooding about how things have gone wrong. He becomes preoccupied with problems. His eyes are now on himself, instead of God. So God calls to him, "Elijah, what are you doing here—hiding in a cave?"

With a pout, Elijah answers, "Lord, the nation is falling apart. The entire government is wicked, immoral. The people have backslidden; they won't even believe in miracles. Society has gone mad. My message has been thrown back in my face. They really don't want help. The devil is in control—he's got everybody but me. I'm the only one left standing true to you, Lord. I'm hiding out to preserve at least one saint."

Elijah, a praying prophet, had been so busy for God, so busy demonstrating God's power, so busy saving God's kingdom, that he became a one-way servant. He had been talking to God often—but doing very little listening. Had he been listening, he would have heard God tell him there were seven thousand saints who had not compromised.

We Need a Lesson on Listening

So God had to teach this servant a lesson on listening. He took him to the very top of Mount Horeb and gave him an illustrated sermon!

> And he said, Go forth, and stand upon the mount before the Lord. And, behold, the Lord passed by, and a great and strong wind rent the mountains, and brake in pieces the rocks before the Lord; but the Lord was not in the wind: and after the wind an earthquake; but the Lord was not in the earthquake: And after the earthquake a fire; but the Lord was not in the fire: and after the fire a still small voice. And it was so, when Elijah heard it, that he wrapped his face in his mantle, and went out, and stood in the entering in of the cave. And, behold, there came a voice unto him, and said, What doest thou here, Elijah?
>
> 1 Kings 19:11–13

When that wind began to howl, I think Elijah thought to himself, "It's about time, Lord. Blow Jezebel right off her throne—throw her and her sinner friends to the winds. Blow them all away! Show Your power!" But God was not in the wind!

Suddenly, a great earthquake—and Elijah said, "That ought to scare them good! God will get even. He will shake them out of their shoes! Thank You, Lord. You are vindicating Your servant." But God was not in the earthquake!

After the earthquake, a fire! The heavens were aglow with white-hot flames! Elijah said to his heart, "Lord, they didn't accept the fire that fell on the altar—burn them out! Burn out wicked Ahab! Fry Jezebel. Cause Your fire to consume the wicked. God, I know You are in this fire!" But God was not in the fire!

. . . and after the fire a still small voice.
1 Kings 19:12

Can you imagine what happened next? A prophet—who was not afraid of a hurricane, who didn't scare at all at an earthquake, who didn't bat an eyelid at heavenly fireworks—is absolutely frightened by a still, small voice. "And it was so, when Elijah heard it, that he wrapped his face in his mantle . . ." (1 Kings 19:13).

Elijah covered his head with his coat! Why? Had not this prophet talked to God many times? Had he not been to the throne seven times on Mount Carmel? Was he not a great man of prayer? Hadn't God used him mightily? Yes! But Elijah was a stranger to the still small voice! He had not allowed "the voice to come to him" (*see* v. 13). He was so wrapped up with spiritual renewal, so wrapped up with an outpouring of rain, so wrapped up sending associates on errands, so wrapped up in a holy cause—he had not waited for the voice!

And when Elijah finally allowed that voice to speak—alone, quiet, away from all the power displays—he got the most specific directions ever in all his ministry to God. "Go to Damascus: go through the wilderness; anoint Hazael king over Syria; anoint Jehu king over Israel; and anoint Elisha to be prophet to follow you" (*see* 1 Kings 19:15, 16).

How many busy, busy children of God today have never had the voice come to them? They are so busy witnessing—going about doing good—praying for a

108

spiritual awakening in the land—fasting—so intense—so sincere—so dedicated. Yet, they have heard everything but the voice of the Lord.

Something Even Better Than Pentecost

John the Baptist never made it to Pentecost! He saw none of the cloven tongues of fire. He did not hear the mighty rushing wind. He did not see Jerusalem shaken and multitudes converted. But John said his joy was fulfilled! He heard something better than the rushing wind, better than good reports, better than the sounds of a joyful bride. He heard the Saviour's voice. "He that hath the bride is the bridegroom: but the friend of the bridegroom, which standeth and heareth him, rejoiceth greatly because of the bridegroom's voice: this my joy therefore is fulfilled" (John 3:29).

John tasted of the greatest joy a follower of Jesus can know. He said, "I stood still, and I heard Him talk to me. His voice made my heart leap. He talked to me personally. I listened to my Lord. And that's my joy. Just hearing His voice."

John could say, "Oh, yes, I loved Him. I talked to Him. I worshiped at His feet. I told Him how unworthy I was. But my joy is not in what I said to Him. My joy is in what He said to me. He spoke to me. I heard His voice, and I rejoice just in the sound of that voice."

Some people teach that the Lord no longer speaks to men, except through the revealed Word. They cannot believe men can be directed and blessed by hearing that still, small voice today.

Jesus said, "My sheep know my voice; they hear when I call . . . another voice they will not hear . . ." (see John 10:3, 4). But, nowadays we are afraid of all the abuses, afraid it will lead to revelations contrary to the Word of God in the Scriptures. But, all the abuses are not God's fault. Every fake vision, false prophecy, false leading is a direct result of man's own pride and self-will. Men abuse every gift of God. Nevertheless, the Lord still speaks directly to the hearts of those waiting to hear.

God, who at sundry times and in divers manners spake in times past unto the fathers by the prophets, Hath in these last days spoken unto us by his Son . . . .

Hebrews 1:1, 2

Wherefore as the Holy Ghost saith, To day if ye will hear his voice, Harden not your hearts . . . .

Hebrews 3:7, 8

His Voice Dispels Loneliness

Millions have been converted and comforted because one man waited to hear His voice. Saul "fell to the earth and heard that voice." And when he became Paul, he kept on hearing that voice. The Lord spoke man-to-man with him. He knew his Shepherd's voice.

Peter allowed the Saviour's voice to come to him. ". . . Peter went up upon the housetop to pray . . . And there came a voice to him . . ." (Acts 10:9, 13). The entire Gentile race was welcomed into the kingdom, along with the house of Cornelius, because a man obeyed a voice. We are living in the same New Testament times as Paul and Peter. We, too, must allow His voice to come to us. "But today, if you will hear His voice . . ." What God could do with Christians who learn to hear from heaven! We could solve most of our problems by simply shutting ourselves in the secret closet to worship and wait. Wait for supernatural advice.

Instead of waiting for His voice to come to us, we run to counselors, to Christian psychologists, to one session after another, reading books, listening to tapes—wanting to hear from God. We want a clear word of direction for our lives! We seek shepherds to dictate our every move. We want pastors to tell us what is right and wrong. We want a leader to follow, a diagram for the future. But few know how to go to the Lord and hear His voice. There are many who know how to get God's attention—to really touch God—but they know nothing about God reaching them. "He that have ears to hear, let him hear" (Matthew 11:15).

God wants to touch the earth once more with the sound of His voice. The whole universe is ready for Holy Ghost directions.

> See that ye refuse not him that speaketh. For if they escaped not who refused him that spake on earth, much more shall not we escape, if we turn away from him that speaketh from heaven: Whose voice then shook the earth: but now he hath promised, saying, Yet once more I shake not the earth only, but also heaven.
>
> Hebrews 12:25, 26

He has promised, "Once again My voice will be heard. Those who hear will inherit the earth. There will come that sure voice that says, 'This is the way, walk ye in it' (Isaiah 30:21). By the hearing of My voice, whatsoever is loosed on earth shall be loosed in heaven."

To the last church, the Laodicean church, the Lord cries, "Behold, I stand at the door, and knock: if any man hear my voice, and open the door, I will come in to him, and will sup with him, and he with me" (Revelation 3:20).

That is the last call of Christ to the church. There will come a spirit of lukewarmness. Luxury will lead to lukewarmness! Multitudes will grow cold. But to His people, He exhorts, "I'm asking to be heard. Open up. Let Me into your secret closet. Let Me talk with you, and you talk with Me. Let's commune. That's how I will keep you from the hour of temptation that is coming on all the world."

The End to All Loneliness—His and Ours

John, in his revelation, talks about a day when our Lord's heart shall be lonely no more. And in His presence, we too shall be lonely no more.

111

And I John saw the holy city, new Jerusalem, coming down from God out of heaven, prepared as a bride adorned for her husband . . . and God himself shall be with them . . . [And God said] I will give unto him that is athirst of the fountain of the water of life freely.

Revelation 21:2, 3, 6

That means free and full communication, with no middle wall of partition; no dark glasses; no knowledge in part; but face-to-face conversation! We think of how glorious it will be to spend an eternity praising our Lord face-to-face, bowing at His knee. But have you ever tried to realize what that great homecoming will mean to our Saviour? All His children home—free to share His every secret. He will make us all sit down, and out of His innermost being will flow rivers of glorious truth. As He did on the road to Emmaus, our Redeemer will begin at Moses and take us all through the prophets. He will share the secrets of the universe. He will unfold every plan. Every cloud of darkness will be dispelled. Christ will share with the redeemed for an eternity!

I see the real joy of heaven as not just ours, but His. Our joy will be that of beholding His joy as He talks to us—to speak freely to us face-to-face. Our greatest joy in heaven will be to see Christ fulfilled—to see His need fully met.

12

Jesus—The Only Cure

Jesus rode into Jerusalem on the back of a donkey. I rode into New York City in a Chevrolet. Jesus came into Jerusalem from the Mount of Olives. I came into New York over the George Washington Bridge.

"And when he was come near, he beheld the city, and wept over it" (Luke 19:41). I know something about that, too! And so does every true minister of the Lord who knows the heart of Jesus. I spent hours riding to my office on the Staten Island Ferry, looking but over the Manhattan skyline, over the junglelike rooftops of Brooklyn, at the thousands of rushing commuters; and I wept!

I wept at nighttime, too—especially when coming in by air to Kennedy Airport and seeing the sprawling lights stretching for miles. It was a sleepless city, with millions headed for hell. I wept because of what I saw wicked men and women doing.

I cried over thousands of young people huddled in dirty apartments, sticking dirty needles into dirty arms. I wept over all the shabbiness, the hollow, empty eyes, the vomiting, the agony and pain, the overdoses.

I wept over the babies born addicted. I could hardly take it, seeing junkie parents carrying sick babies up and down the streets, begging for a few dollars for "medicine for my sick baby." And then, seeing them hand the baby to some other junkie friend, going to the pusher, and getting a fix for themselves. Babies in hospitals, kicking the habit they inherited from the bloodstream of their mothers, made me weep. Sure, I wept; anyone would.

I wept because of the little four-year-old boy found

113

abandoned at the midtown bus station. His mother purposely let go of his hand in the rush hour and left him screaming. I wept when I saw where they took him—to the children's shelter in Manhattan—where hundreds of unwanted children were herded in like a bunch of cattle. It's agonizing at Christmastime, to see them looking out the windows at you, going about doing your Christmas shopping, while they waste away without love. It's a crime, and it makes one weep!

I wept over what I saw in that old, ugly, New York jail called The Tombs! It's a horrible sight to see ten to fifteen young men, all handcuffed, being pushed and clubbed out of a paddy wagon through those ugly gates. It's a nightmare even to visit there: sweaty, crowded, dirty, no air, no sunlight—just a mass of human bodies locked up like a crowded pack of animals. You keep seeing your son locked up in there. And, you cry!

You cry with the mothers, trying to protect little babies in rat-infested ghettos. I'll never forget the many times I've wept over the sight of rat bites on babies—of light bulbs hanging on cords to keep rats from crawling over babies in the middle of the night—of opening any cabinet to see hundreds of roaches running in all directions.

You cry when you walk into an apartment and find two little children sitting on a sofa like little, frightened rabbits, holding hands and softly whimpering. Their junkie parents leave them days at a time. You see a quart of spoiled milk and a box of cookies on the table. You weep about the fear you see in their eyes. You weep when you think of the hopeless future they face.

Yes, we have all wept over a city: over the neglected thousands of elderly people who die forgotten and unwanted in the welfare homes; over little girls who get raped and beaten; over alcoholics lying out on cold Bowery streets and dying like dogs; over slumlords who drive Cadillacs past the filthy tenements they rent at eye-gouging prices; over all those big, rich, downtown churches that own half the city, which invest millions in

Wall Street and let the poor live like pigs.

And if all this weeping I've been talking about seems compassionate and Christlike, remember this: It was not the problems that made Christ weep. Christ did not weep over Jerusalem for the same reasons I wept over New York. Of course, Jesus' concern for their problems is greater than ours, but something else makes Him weep the most.

Jesus wept over what people were not doing. They were not coming to Him for the solution to all that city's problems. He wept because they did not recognize Him. Jesus called it a "wicked and adulterous generation." He knew the city was filled with dead men's bones, covered with whitewash. He knew it was filled with divorce, murder, covetousness, stealing, disobedience to parents, unnatural affection. He knew the streets were crowded with men who loved pleasure more than God, and that the multitudes were fulfilling the lusts of the flesh.

He knew what was going on in religious circles, all in the name of God—hypocrites, Pharisees, a temple of money changers deceiving the multitudes. The houses of prayer had been turned into dens of robbers and thieves. He knew all about the harlots, the alcoholics who lingered at the cup, the cheating merchants with the unjust scales, the gouging moneylenders, the corrupt judges, the blaspheming, cursing mobs.

But these were not the things that made the Saviour weep! He wept at what they did not do—at what they did not see—at what they did not know! "If thou hadst known, even thou, at least in this thy day, the things which belong unto thy peace! but now they are hid from thine eyes" (Luke 19:42).

The cheering crowds thought He wept for joy because of their hosannas and praises! They must have seen Him weeping loud and desperately and said, "Look, He is overwhelmed at the reception this city is giving Him. He is overcome to the point of tears. It must be the sight of all the waving branches, the garments strewn across His

115

path. Those are tears of triumph."

Not so! The heart of Jesus was broken because of the spiritual blindness all around Him! He wanted to do so much for them in their time while He was near, but they would not believe! He promised them rest, yet they continued in their anxiety and restlessness! He promised peace, and they preferred to live in strife. He wanted to be their Shepherd, yet they wandered like sheep having no shepherd. They were hungry and thirsty, but they would not come to Him and be satisfied.

What a tragedy! The answer to every problem of every person in that city was right in their midst, but they didn't take advantage of it! His words were not taken seriously! His offers were not accepted! He came unto His own, and His own received Him not!

In my mind, I see the Son of God, riding on that donkey down the streets of Jerusalem, and I want to run ahead of Him screaming, "Hey, all you sinners, look to the Lamb of God. He's your friend. He loves you! He has the power to set you free right now. Go up to Him, tell Him you believe in Him; confess your sins to Him. You can be free and at peace!" I'd run into the courthouse and scream, "Hey, all you unhappy fathers and mothers, look who's coming down the street on that donkey—the Healer of homes! He hates divorce, but He loves you! Go tell Him all about it. He has a solution. You can start all over again." I'd run into the schoolhouse and scream, "Hey, all you young people! Come see the Man who knows all about you; the Son of God is passing this way. Look! He is the source of all life. Go to Him, touch Him, give yourself to Him. He won't turn you down. He loves children, young people. He'll tell you what you need. He'll be your perfect guide."

I'd want to spread the word about, who He was and the power He had, to everyone I saw. I would scream and weep, "What's wrong with all you people here in Jerusalem? Don't you know who this man is? He won't be here long; time is short. He has all power. Can't you see how blind you are? Don't you know this is your hour of visitation?''·

But this generation is just as blind. We still break the heart of Jesus. He weeps over us, even more than He must have wept over Jerusalem. Jesus knew we would have more sin than Jerusalem. He knew evil men would wax worse and worse! He knew hell would spill over its boundaries. He knew Satan would fall on the earth with wrath, that demon powers would be unleashed. He knew there would be terrible pressures on the family, that crime would get worse, that lust and sensuality would seduce many, that parents and children would betray one another, that drugs and alcohol would take their toll. He knew that suicides would become pandemic. And that is why He promised more grace! More power! Better promises! Greater works! He knew we would need it.

Jesus wept publicly before, at Lazarus' tomb, because even His friends forgot who He was and what He had promised. He had told them He was the resurrection and the life, and all they could say was, ''It's too late.'' Through His tears, He must have been saying to the Father, ''Why is it so hard for them to take Me at My word? Why don't they listen to what I say? Why are they so blind about Me? What do I have to do to prove to them I have been given all power?''

We don't seem to understand Jesus today, any more than they did in Jerusalem. We are as blind to His power as those other friends of His at the tomb of Lazarus!

Jerusalem was a city in turmoil. It was headed for Judgment. Jesus prophesied, ''Enemies will surround you; you will be laid even with the ground. Not one stone will be left upon another. Your children will be destroyed.''

He saw the crime, the restlessness, the coming Judgment, and He cried out, ''I wanted to heal you; I wanted to give you rest! I wanted to solve your problems. I wanted to guide you. Like a mother hen gathers her chicks, I wanted to take you under my wings, to love you, to be your Saviour. But, you would have nothing to do with it. You don't even know what you have turned down. You don't have the slightest idea of all you are missing.''

So it is today. Jesus sees all the unrest in our land, the divorce, the drinking, the drugs, the despair, the loneliness. He sees the tragic wave of suicide, and once again our Lord weeps over a generation. ''Why are you so blind? Why can't you see what I have offered you? Why won't you take me at my word? Why don't you recognize your hour of visitation? Why do you live with such problems when you have so many great and precious promises?''

Jesus said of the multitudes in Jerusalem, ''You would not.'' How could that be? Were they not lining the streets singing His praises? Thousands in that city were calling Him King! They were dancing and shouting. That would be like having Jesus attend one of the great religious conventions in our time, with thousands raising their hands, singing His praises, calling Him Lord, Lord—and then hearing Him weep and cry, ''Why won't you see? Why can't you understand what is really yours? You are living so far beneath what I've promised you.''

You see, it's quite easy to get people excited about Jesus. It's easy to promote shouting, praising, and hosannas. It's quite another thing to get those shouting people to really take Him at His Word and appropriate it to everyday problems.

Who really breaks His heart? The junkie, the harlot, the rapist, the murderer? No! His heart is broken by people who praise Him with their lips, but who, in action and deed, do not take Him at His Word. They do not claim His promises! They go through life pretending; they go on living in despair—living in fear, divorcing, blundering through life with restlessness, and finally killing themselves.

Let me tell you who I believe breaks His heart the most. The one who turns down His friendship and His offer to help. He offers Himself as a Friend to sinners. He was gladly known as "a friend of sinners." He made His friendship easy and uncomplicated, so that even a little child could understand. He understands those suicidal urges.

Jesus looks over this world, weeping and crying out, "Why can't you see that all I want to be is your Friend? I want to break the chains, bring you back to peace and rest. I won't harm you; I won't force Myself on you. I want to fill that empty place in your life."

If you are lost, you have a Friend! The greatest tragedy on earth is that people He is trying so hard to reach, whom He is wanting so much to help, won't accept that friendship. Christ weeps because His offer of love is rejected—ignored! His promises are left unclaimed. He weeps because we have so much need, and He has so much to give, and we will not take it. He will weep over many right now who are reading this message, who will again turn down His offer.

Through His tears, He is begging to heal every home, to mend every broken heart, to heal every hurt, to renew love lost, to make all things new. Pastors tell me their congregations are now gripped by a wave of divorce, separation, and family troubles. They are counseling more and more people who are ready to give up on life. They talk about suicide without flinching.

Suicide is an epidemic, even among Christians, and it gets worse day by day. How it must break His heart to see so-called believers carry His Holy Word, have three or four versions of every promise clearly revealed, hear the preaching of His Word, then go about their way as if it meant nothing. Jesus said, "And all things, whatsoever ye shall ask in prayer, believing, ye shall receive" (Matthew 21:22). "If ye shall ask any thing in my name, I will do it" (John 14:14).

But we act as though we really do not believe a word of it. We refuse to take hold of those promises. We must not really want them! We run to Christian psychiatrists; we

119

read books; and we go to counselors. By our actions, we prove we really have no faith in His Word. And that is why His heart is broken. He wants your family healed. He wants you to live in joy and peace. He wants you to enter His rest! But, ". . . we will not . . ."

We are like the four leprous men who sat outside the gates of Samaria, dying in their despair. The city was ravaged by famine, and all hope was gone. But just a short distance away stood an empty Syrian camp, loaded with tons of food, barrels of water, empty tents for shelter, and countless horses and chariots. There was gold, silver, and raiment in abundance. Desperation drove them into that empty camp, and what a discovery they made. All they needed, and more, was there all the time.

Our Lord has provided us with a storehouse loaded with benefits. He has given us great and precious promises, to cover every emergency of life. He has given His Word, to supply every need and answer every desperate call. Why, then, do we sit around in our despair, searching for some other way out? Why do we read book after book, and go from place to place, asking question after question—when all along, our answer is simply in coming directly to Jesus for everything?

It is a serious matter for Christians to get away from simple, childlike faith and begin to lean on the arm of flesh. Not only do you hurt yourself in the process, you also break the Master's heart. You make Him weep, because He is more anxious to give than you are to receive, but you will not come for shelter under His wing. You are still running around in the storms of life, unprotected and uncovered.

It will be a brokenhearted Saviour who stands to judge the world on that final day. As a child, I conjured pictures in my mind about how it would be on Judgment Day: A great white throne, before which are gathered the multitudes from every race and color. Death and hell would deliver up the dead, and every human ever born would stand before that throne to be judged. The books would be opened, and all would be judged according to their works.

What is recorded in those books to be opened on the Judgment Day? Is it a documented list of every lie, every act of adultery, every evil thought, every drunken night spent in debauchery? Is it an account of all the hates, the prejudices, the cheating, and the dishonesty men have been guilty of? No! I believe it is much more than that. It is not enough that sinners be forced to face every evil deed done in the flesh.

I believe we will be judged not so much for what we have done as for what we have not done. We will be judged for rejecting the love of Jesus. What Christ said through His tears to the city of Jerusalem, He will say to every human who stands before Him on Judgment Day: "All I wanted to do was gather you under My wings. I wanted to be your Friend, to guide and protect you. I wanted to shield you from the storms of life. I wanted to be your way out of every difficulty. But you would not! You refused My offer of love."

Friends, that will be the terror of hell. I can't bring myself to believe God is nearly as interested in your fleshly habits as He is in your rejection of His love.

In those books will be a documented list of every sermon you have ever heard, of every Bible verse you have ever read. There will be the exact dates and times you heard television evangelists preaching Christ's love; a list of every meeting you have attended; a notation about every twinge of conviction, of every call of the Spirit, of every claim God ever made on your soul. Your sins of the flesh hurt only you, but your rejection hurts Him. That is the judgment. You broke His heart and threw His love back in His face. There are no words in any language that can describe the terror that awaits those who, once and for all, reject His free offer of love and grace.

Turn to Jesus in your hour of need. Confess your sins to Him, honestly. Then open your heart to receive His love and forgiveness. Commit your future into His care, because He really does care for you.

You don't have to die in darkness and fear. You can be set free and live a life of real joy and perfect peace. You can stake your very life on this single promise:

For God so loved the world, that he gave his only begotten Son, that whosoever believeth in him should not perish, but have everlasting life.

John 3:16

For further information or counseling, please write—

David Wilkerson Crusades
Route 1, Box 80
Lindale, Texas 75771

WHAT DOES THE BIBLE SAY ABOUT THE
END TIMES?
Don't You Think You Should Find Out?

____ **THE TERMINAL GENERATION,** Hal Lindsey, $1.95
In a chaotic, confused world that yearns for authenticity and validity, only the Bible remains as a constant source of hope and direction.

____ **RACING TOWARD JUDGMENT,** David Wilkerson, $1.50
Be aware of the signs that foretell the Judgment Day.

____ **ANTICHRIST AFTER THE OMEN,** Frank Allnutt, $1.75
Learn the truth about the Satanic mission of the Antichrist, and how you can prepare for his coming.

____ **THE LAST DAYS OF MAN,** Bill Petersen, $1.75
Although humanity faces an unprecedented crisis, the Christian knows that these final days are actually a new beginning.

____ **THE KING AND YOU,** Bob Mumford, $1.75
The kingdom of Jesus Christ is coming and will revolutionize your life!

Order From Your Bookstore

If your bookstore does not stock these books, order from
SPIRE BOOKS
Box 150, Old Tappan, New Jersey 07675

Please send me the books I've checked above. Enclosed is my payment plus 35¢ mailing charge on first book ordered, 10¢ each additional book.

Name _____

Street_____

City _____ State_____ Zip_____

_____ Amount enclosed ____Cash ____Check ____Money order
(No C.O.D.'s)